Martíneztown, 1945

Querencias Series
Miguel A. Gandert and Enrique R. Lamadrid, Series Editors

Querencia is a popular term in the Spanish-speaking world that is used to express a deeply rooted love of place and people. This series promotes a transnational, humanistic, and creative vision of the US-Mexico borderlands based on all aspects of expressive culture, both material and intangible.

Also available in the Querencias Series:

Where the North Ends: A Novel by Hugo Moreno
Dichos en Nichos by Sage Vogel
The Latino Big Bang in California: The Diary of Justo Veytia, a Mexican Forty-Niner edited by David E. Hayes-Bautista, Cynthia L. Chamberlin, and Paul Bryan Gray
New Mexico's Moses: Reies López Tijerina and the Religious Origins of the Mexican American Civil Rights Movement by Ramón A. Gutiérrez
The Poetics of Fire: Metaphors of Chile Eating in the Borderlands by Victor M. Valle
El Camino Real de California: From Ancient Pathways to Modern Byways by Joseph P. Sánchez
Chasing Dichos through Chimayó by Don J. Usner
Nación Genízara: Ethnogenesis, Place and Identity in New Mexico edited by Moises Gonzales and Enrique R. Lamadrid
Querencia: Reflections on the New Mexico Homeland edited by Vanessa Fonseca-Chávez, Levi Romero, and Spencer R. Herrera
Imagine a City That Remembers: The Albuquerque Rephotography Project by Anthony Anella and Mark C. Childs

For additional titles in the Querencias Series, please visit unmpress.com.

Martíneztown, 1945

Tales of Life and Loss in an Albuquerque Barrio

Nasario García

UNIVERSITY OF NEW MEXICO PRESS | ALBUQUERQUE

Printed in the United States of America

Library of Congress Cataloging-in-Publication Data
Names: García, Nasario, author.
Title: Martíneztown, 1945: tales of life and loss in an Albuquerque barrio / Nasario García.
Other titles: Albuquerque: the day I shed a tear | Querencias series.
Description: Albuquerque: University of New Mexico Press, 2025. |
Series: Querencias series
Identifiers: LCCN 2025006777 (print) | LCCN 2025006778 (ebook) |
ISBN 9780826368669 (paperback) | ISBN 9780826368676 (epub)
Subjects: LCSH: García, Nasario—Homes and haunts. | García, Nasario—Childhood and youth. | Martinez Town (N.M.) | Albuquerque (N.M.)—Biography—Anecdotes. | Albuquerque (N.M.)—Social life and customs—20th century. | Albuquerque (N.M.)—History—20th century.
Classification: LCC F804.A3 G373 2025 (print) | LCC F804.A3 (ebook) |
DDC 978.961—dc23/eng/20250217
LC record available at https://lccn.loc.gov/2025006777
LC ebook record available at https://lccn.loc.gov/2025006778

Founded in 1889, the University of New Mexico sits on the traditional homelands of the Pueblo of Sandia. The original peoples of New Mexico—Pueblo, Navajo, and Apache—since time immemorial have deep connections to the land and have made significant contributions to the broader community statewide. We honor the land itself and those who remain stewards of this land throughout the generations and also acknowledge our committed relationship to Indigenous peoples. We gratefully recognize our history.

Cover photograph courtesy of author
Designed by Felicia Cedillos
Composed in Chapparral Pro

LONGSTANDING FRIENDSHIPS

V. B. "Barrett" Price, a wonderful human being,
a remarkable poet,

and

Sue Boggio, a delightful person and superb novelist

The nice thing about preserving memories . . .
is that they don't have an expiration date!

—ZIGGY AND FRIENDS, INC. DISTRIBUTED BY ANDREWS MCMEEL

Whether by mere happenstance, good luck or misfortune,
one goes where destiny beckons you.

—NASARIO GARCÍA

CONTENTS

ACKNOWLEDGMENTS

At the onset I wish to express my sincere appreciation to Sonia Dickey, acquisitions editor, for her professional guidance in seeing the present work brought to light. My personal thanks go as well to James Ayers, editorial, design, and production manager; Isaac Morris, designer; Anna Pohlod, editor; Don Redpath, sales and marketing manager; and Sarena Ulibarri, publicist. A word of recognition is hereby expressed to Min Marcus, production assistant, for all of the foregoing at the University of New Mexico Press. A special word of gratitude also goes to Enrique Lamadrid, editor of the Querencias Series for his total support. Lastly, many thanks go to Patricia Kot, copyeditor and proofreader, for her excellent editorial suggestions.

INTRODUCTION

Martíneztown, 1945: Tales of Life and Loss in an Albuquerque Barrio is a compilation of personal recollections that take the reader to Albuquerque's Santa Barbara / Martíneztown neighborhood at the end of World War II. Innocent, hapless, heart-rending, and kind human beings in my adopted community inspired the accounts herein.

The leadoff story, "The Day I Shed a Tear," dramatizes how a pack of dogs mauled my dog, Chopo, to death as I headed for Santa Barbara School (constructed in the early 1900s, today a historic site). Distraught at the loss of my beloved pet I yearned to return to the family ranch in the Río Puerco Valley.

Let us go back in time. After the demise of the WPA (Workers Progress Administration) during the early 1940s, my father, like many other ranchers and farmers in the Río Puerco Valley southeast of Chaco Canyon where we lived, lost his job. To make matters worse, he struggled to carve out an existence from the land on his parents' ranch to feed a growing family. The skies had become increasingly frugal with their clouds and precipitation. Not even the *santos* seemed to heed my mother's supplications for rain to sprinkle the crops.

The pressures of living on the fringes were mounting for Mom and Dad. The time to take stock not so much of our past, but of our present with a future in mind, preoccupied them. Our past was clear, our present very much in the balance, and our future as murky as the muddy waters of the Río Puerco. In their best wisdom my parents decided to move to Albuquerque in the hope of a better life. My father, an extremely intelligent man with only a fifth-grade education and no technical training whatsoever, was determined to carve out a new niche for the entire family.

The sultry days of July 1945, as my family and I ventured into Albuquerque, are still embedded in my psyche. But what made those summer days memorable was not the heat. More striking was the change from the open spaces in rural New Mexico to a new and confined existence in quasi-urban life in the so-called Duke City. Throughout time I learned to adapt to, as well as to cope with, a variety of surprising external forces.

We relocated to the Hispanic barrio of Santa Barbara (named after the Santa Barbara Cemetery founded in 1869), although most local citizens considered it an integral part of Martíneztown,* a historic enclave in what was then northeast Albuquerque. Our new abode—if one could graciously call it that—was my paternal grandmother's *dispensa*, a storage shed on my grandparents' home west of the Santa Barbara Cemetery. Grandma Lale's forlorn shed stood in their back yard as if to convey its own sympathy upon our arrival. The tattered screen door, the only entrance to the tiny dwelling, greeted us with the clearly visible words that read "RAINBO is Good Bread." My little brother Beltrán, six years old, with a penchant for cutting up even at his age said, "*Amá, aquí vamos estar toos atoraos como gallinas.*" (Mom, we're going to be stuck here like chickens.) He had spoken volumes.

Our cramped quarters for two adults and five children (a sister was born here later) for the next four unforgettable, tense, and unpredictable years (1945–1949) was the first contradiction or anomaly. But for the moment, at least, the present reality was an eye-opener to my mother, first and foremost. As for my father's reaction to our current situation, it was all a matter of the end

* For a treatise on Martíneztown I recommend *Martíneztown 1823–1950: Hispanics, Italians, Jesuits & Land Investors in New Town Albuquerque* by Joseph P. Sánchez & Larry D. Miller.

justifying the means. "Nothing lasts forever," were his consoling words. Years later we moved to Los Ranchos de Alburquerque. There Dad built Mom a home with adobes that he purchased from our neighbor Daniel Sedillo in Los Ranchos, who hailed from Martíneztown.

For a young boy like me, Santa Barbara opened my eyes to the allure, travails, and disappointments of a semi-urban life in Albuquerque. Though life as a child can be adventurous, I somehow found the beginning of our new existence bizarre and eerie, which left me to ponder if survival in the vicissitudes of the inner city was even or ever possible. The strangeness I felt in a so-called barrio was not only ratified but in some cases magnified at Santa Barbara School.[†] A number of students treated me like a country bumpkin. While not prepared to cope with those unknown forces, I was determined above all not to succumb to kids' tomfoolery or teasing just so they could claim victory or another victim.

Bit by bit I became exposed to a confined world that clashed dramatically with the blue skies and wide-open spaces of my beloved Río Puerco Valley. The unlimited freedom I once relished in the countryside was now reduced to square footage and a fenced yard where you could reach across to your neighbor's house and touch the walls plastered with cement, not mud. Even the homes on our street somehow seemed to be lined up one after the other like chickens roosting in the chicken coop.

Pumping water from Grandma Lale's pump was also a novelty. So, too, was running errands to the small privately owned neighborhood stores or carrying our trash weekly to the city's garbage dump. Today this area lies parallel to Interstate 25, not far from the so-called Big I that links the North and South I-25 with I-40, east and west.

† Anyone interested in my education and career in academia, I recommend *Beyond My Adobe Schoolhouse: My Life in Education*, University of New Mexico Press. Visit my website: https://nasariogarcia.com.

I did relate to a handful of things in Santa Barbara. For example, virtually every family had an outhouse. On Mondays, wash day, women hung their clothes to dry on a clothesline. And the ever-present chimneys spewed plumes of white and dark smoke from the wood-burning stoves. For good measure one could add poverty, pride, hardworking men and women, and Spanish, the people's dominant language.

A prime example of the rural and urban worlds that merge or clash is seen in "Wanna Go to the Movies?" The lighthearted story calls to mind my first-ever visit to a movie theater in downtown Albuquerque. Pat Perea, a neighbor whom I befriended, and his pals burst out laughing when I hid under my seat upon seeing a herd of galloping horses on the screen coming toward me. I thought I was going to be trampled to death.

Some of the words and expressions my barrio friends employed as they ambled to and from the theater baffled me. Their mode of communication, esoteric at best, becomes more vivid in "Borrego." Borrego is a zoot-suiter whose inner-city jargon clashes with my own standard and regional Spanish of the countryside.

Time and again the reader will encounter colorful and intriguing characters in *Martíneztown, 1945, Tales of Life and Loss in an Albuquerque Barrio*. A case in point is the inimitable drunkard Tranquilino (aka el Tanque/the Tank) highlighted in "The Man Who Swore a Lot." He is renowned for his plethora of obscenities directed, above all, against women. An antithesis in temperament can be seen in the generous bachelor don Hilario, as portrayed in "Don Hilario and His Hogs." He hosts a yearly Matanza in the fall and invites his neighbors to join in the traditional festivity of butchering and sharing a pig.

Language and culture are mutually inclusive, for one cannot exist without the other. Don Hilario is emblematic of both. He, like his neighbors who migrated to Santa Barbara, steadily adjusted to the trials and tribulations of urban life but did not assimilate completely.

The characters mentioned above reflect in part the captivating personalities the reader will encounter in *Martíneztown, 1945: Tales of Life and Loss in an Albuquerque Barrio*. I first wrote my remembrances in Spanish, my native tongue, even though my ancestral roots stretch across several centuries in New Mexico. The use of Spanish is pivotal since it drives the theme, tone, and development of the respective characters within each story, as well as in the English version.

As translator, one must be conscious of the spirit and nuances inherent in the target language. This is especially true in translating plays on words, double meanings, or idiomatic expressions. Each one of these entities must be treated with flexibility otherwise the conversion from Spanish to English loses its flair and authenticity. The art of translating is not a perfect science, to be sure, therefore maintaining the integrity of language and culture as much as humanly possible is fundamental.

A bilingual glossary juxtaposing regional terms with those of modern usage, plus common expressions or idioms, have been included for readers who are unfamiliar with the northern New Mexican Spanish dialect. Zoot-suiter expressions or *pachuquismos* typical among inner-city youth during the 1940s are appended as well.

Seventy-plus years have passed since my family and I left Santa Barbara/Martíneztown for Los Ranchos de Alburquerque. My grandparents, Teodoro and Emilia García (nicknamed Lolo and Lale, respectively), bought their Santa Barbara home in 1912, the year my father was born. Located at 417 Wilson Avenue (today Aspen Avenue), it still stands. Though the home was sold shortly after my grandparents' death in 1972, I nonetheless visit the neighborhood from time to time.

But those days of yore are gone and etched only in memory: cars have replaced people strolling to and fro; dirt roads where kids played are now paved; and the nameless back alleys of yesteryear today boast the names of proud folks who have gone on to a better life. Even the gurgling ditch built around 1830 that once ran through the barrio when my family and I lived in Santa Barbara in the 1940s no longer exists. Nowadays everything seems eerily peaceful in comparison to the hustle and bustle of the barrio that I hereby describe in *Martíneztown, 1945: Tales of Life and Loss in an Albuquerque Barrio*.

I am pleased to pay homage, individually and collectively, to those private citizens of bygone years. Regardless of their character traits or shortcomings, real or invented, they were decent human beings whom I observed day in and day out. Above all else, every single individual—fictional or non-fictional—in the ensuing stories demonstrates his or her own *raison d'être* whether victim, hero, or *persona non grata*.

NASARIO GARCÍA, PHD
Santa Fe, New Mexico

The Day I Shed a Tear

MY BELOVED DOG'S NAME was Chopo. He was the first and only dog I ever had as a kid. Because of the hurtful and ugly way that he died I never had the desire to talk about him until now.

Let us turn back the clock. I was six years old when Dad gave Chopo to me at our ranch in the Río Puerco Valley of New Mexico where my family and I lived. As a kid, time is something I took for granted. Time only mattered when I got hungry, sleepy, or my playing time was cut short because of having to do household or ranch chores. Otherwise, time came and went routinely like the four yearly seasons.

More than seventy years have passed since I became the proud owner of Chopo, a beautiful beige-and-white puppy. He was my loyal companion for three years. As he got older, Chopo playfully chased after Mom's chickens. He was good-natured. I loved him very much.

At first Mom let him sleep on the floor in the bedroom but only because he was a puppy and the nights were cold. Once the weather turned warm, Chopo had to stay outside. One day when I least expected it, Mom popped a question.

"*Hijito*, my dear son, have you thought of a name for your little dog? You can't keep calling him '*perrito* (puppy dog).' You have to baptize him," Mom said, and she winked at me.

"Like when my little sister was baptized at the church?"

"Well, not exactly, but you should give him a name. Animals

enjoy names just like us humans. That's why your dad named his horse El Moro, which means bluish-gray."

I didn't have a clue what to name my puppy until one morning before breakfast. I hopped out of bed but I couldn't fine my house slippers. This was not the first time I had looked and looked for them. I usually found my puppy playing with them under the bed. Suddenly a name clicked.

"Guess what, Mom?" I said to her, all excited, as I finished my oatmeal. "I'm going to name my little dog Chopo,"

"Why Chopo?" Mom asked.

"Because every time I go looking for my *chopos* (house shoes), one is missing. That's why I want to baptize him Chopo," I said, and Mom smiled as I looked at her.

"I think that's a clever idea and a good name for your puppy," Mom added. "Your father will be very proud of you."

That evening Dad came home from work. While we were eating supper, Mom broke the silence.

"Hijito, aren't you going to tell your dad the good news?"

"What good news?" I answered, somewhat confused.

"You know, about your dog."

"Oh yes!" I said, trying to collect my thoughts. "Dad, I have something to tell you."

"You do? And what is it?" he asked before I could continue.

"I now have a name for my puppy. From now on we're going to call him Chopo."

"Chopo! How did you come up with a name like that?" I then gave him the same explanation that I had given Mom.

"Hijito, that's a good name. I like it. The kids in our neighborhood will love the name Chopo."

"What neighborhood?" I exclaimed in a loud voice.

Dad's words hit me like a good kick in the stomach. I didn't know what he was talking about. Mom had not said anything to me either about leaving the ranch.

"*Mijo*," Dad said to me in a serious tone of voice, "we're leaving the ranch and moving to Alburquerque where I'll try to find a job to feed the family. That is no longer possible here on our small ranch. In September you'll go to a school in the city."

We moved to the Santa Barbara barrio. I wasn't too thrilled about going to a new school. I started at Santa Barbara Elementary School. It wasn't very far from my paternal grandparents' storage room, where we now lived, so I walked. That first day I ate breakfast and then went outside to look for Chopo. I hollered at him; he was lying under Dad's old clunker, *carrito*.

"Chopo. *Ven a comer. Tengo que irme a la escuela.*" (Come and eat. I have to leave for school.) By now he answered to his name. I gave him something to eat and he gobbled it all up.

"*Bueno, ya me voy*" (Okay, I'm going), and I rubbed his head. He wiggled his tail; he was happy.

I went inside the house to say goodbye to Mom. When I came out, Chopo was at the entrance waiting for me.

"*Bueno, hasta la tarde amá.*" (Okay, see you this afternoon, Mom.)

I hurried because I didn't want to be late for my first day of school. When I crossed Edith Boulevard alongside Santa Barbara Cemetery just before I got to school, I heard a voice.

"Hey, doggie. You going to *eschool*? *Whatsa* matter? Can't you *speek Inglish*?" said a young boy who was bouncing a basketball on his way to school. I looked back and saw Chopo.

"*Chopo, ¿qué haces aquí?*" (What are you doing here?)

"Hey! What's *jour naime*? And don't *jour* dog *speek Inglish*?" I heard the boy again but I ignored him. "I *esked ju* something. *Eez dat jour* dog? *¿Tu perro?*"

"Yes," I responded. "He don't understand you. He only *espeeks* Espanish."

"Well, he *betta* learn to *speek Inglish* like the dogs in the barrio," he said to me in a threatening manner. At that given moment this other boy came up to me.

"You better keep an eye on your dog," he cautioned me, "'cause there's some mean dogs around."

"And who are you?" I asked.

"I'm Bobby Ortega. I live two doors from your grandma."

I got Chopo by the collar and took him home as quickly as possible. Mom tied him to the car porch, and then I ran back to school as fast as I could. I didn't want to be late.

Santa Barbara School had several rooms for different grades and teachers. This was a contrast to the one-room schoolhouse used for grades one to eight back at the ranch, and only one teacher.

That day, the kids in the school grounds made fun of my bib overalls and high-top shoes. They also poked fun at how I spoke what little English I knew and the way I said certain words with a Spanish accent. My classmates were not very kind either, but somehow I endured my first day of school.

When I got home Chopo was under Dad's car, his favorite resting place. As soon as he saw me, he ran toward me.

"*Epa, Chopo. ¿Qué tal?*" (Hey, Chopo. What's up?)

I rubbed his head, and he wiggled his tail. He was tickled to see me, and I was happy to see him as well. Mom heard the noise and came out the kitchen door to greet me.

"Hijito, you're home! How was school? I bet you had fun, right?"

"Well, yes and no," I responded with little enthusiasm. "Those *atascaos*, dimwitted school kids laughed at my English."

"Don't be bitter, hijito. Nothing lasts forever. And remember, 'On this earth it is better to forget about insults than to seek vengeance.'"

"Okay, Mom," and I left it at that. I didn't dare tell her about kids making fun of my pants and shoes.

My second day of school was better, but on my third day, instead of coming home for lunch, Mom wrapped scrambled eggs with fried potatoes in a flour tortilla. I carried my lunch in a brown paper sack and ate it in the cafeteria where lots of kids ate hot lunches. A couple kids from my class joined me, but when they saw what I was eating, they laughed, made a snide remark, and left. I didn't tell Mom anything about this incident.

The next day she fixed me a sandwich of fried zucchini and corn wrapped in a flour tortilla that I had always liked. But instead of taking it with me to school, I fed it to Chopo (without Mom seeing me, of course) before I left for school. I didn't want kids to make fun of my lunch again.

My third day at school was uneventful, but by the time I got home, I was very hungry. Mom was sitting in her chair in front of the shed holding my baby sister, Elsie. Mom had a sad look on her face.

"Mom, what's wrong?"

"Hijito, go look at Chopo. There's something wrong with him," she said to me in a vague sort of way.

"What? What?" I reacted, scared to death.

At first I thought that maybe my zucchini and corn sandwich was the culprit, but as I approached Chopo, who was lying on the dirt under Dad's carrito, I knew it had to be something more serious. I crawled toward him. He was listless. Immediately, I noticed that his ears were all chewed up and bleeding.

"Chopo, Chopo, what is wrong? What happened to you? Who did this to you?"

He moaned and groaned. I dared not touch his head but I did caress his belly. The palm of my hand soaked quickly from the blood oozing from his ribs. I got sick to my stomach and started to cry and to vomit. Mom got down on her knees and saw how distraught I was. She tried to comfort me.

"Mom, what happened to Chopo? Do you know?"

"Hijito, Chopo evidently followed you to school but along the way was attacked by a pack of dogs. Our neighbor don Melitón across the street from us heard a commotion in the street. He tried to rescue Chopo from the dogs, but it was too late. Chopo somehow was able to walk home. Don Melitón followed him. He's the one who told me about the pack of dogs."

"Mom, is Chopo going to be all right or not?"

"Who knows, hijito? It's all in God's hands."

She left me alone with Chopo. I watched him carefully. Soon I began to see his stomach heaving more and more. I talked to him, but he seemed to be having trouble breathing. This lasted for a few minutes. Suddenly his body shook and went motionless. I put my ear to his stomach the way Grandpa did when his horse died back at the ranch. Chopo was no longer breathing. My beloved dog died quietly before my eyes. A profound loneliness came over me. I felt all alone. I felt empty inside. I had lost my good friend. What would I do without him?

I went inside the house and told Mom. I couldn't stop crying. She hugged me and tried her best to ease my pain.

"Mom," I said to her, "I wish we had never come to this neighborhood. Not even the dogs like us. I want to go back to the ranch."

Right at that moment Dad got home from work and saw me crying.

"What's going on? Is something wrong?" he asked, with a puzzled look on his face. "Why are you sobbing?"

"Chopo has died," Mom interjected. "A pack of brutal dogs attacked him and mauled him to death. Go see for yourself. He's under the car."

"Dad, what are we going to do now? What are we going to do with Chopo? We can't leave him under the car."

"We shall bury him."

"But where?"

"Tomorrow is Saturday and I don't have to work. We'll take him to the garbage dump. That's where we'll bury him."

That night I couldn't sleep a wink. I tossed and turned all night long. I kept thinking about Chopo and how much I was going to miss him. After breakfast, my dad and I loaded Chopo in my little red wagon that he and Mom had given me for Christmas.

"Dad, how far is the *dompe*?" I asked.

"Not too far. We'll be there in no time at all. It's by the cemetery. You see that smoke up ahead? That's where we're going."

As we walked through the neighborhood, people looked at us.

They could see that we were carrying a dead dog. They no doubt wondered what had happened, but we weren't in any mood to tell them, even if they had asked. When we reached the dump, I saw several heaps of trash. One was smoldering. It was not a pretty sight. All of a sudden a man emerged mysteriously from behind a dark cloud of smoke.

"What can I do for you?" he asked my dad.

"My son's dog died and we came to bury him."

"Sorry. We don't bury dead animals here," he remarked in a cold and heartless manner. "Just leave it here. I'll take care of him," he added in a gruff voice.

Dad and I carefully unloaded Chopo from my wagon and placed him on the ground next to some cardboard boxes that read BIG HUNK CANDY. I gave Chopo an affectionate pat on the head, said goodbye, and walked away with tears in my eyes.

"Wait a minute," Dad said to me. "Let's load Chopo back on your wagon. We're not going to leave him here in a bunch of garbage. We'll take him home."

His words totally surprised me since Dad rarely showed much emotion.

"Dad, what are we going to do with Chopo? There's no place to bury him at Grandpa and Grandma's backyard."

"Not to worry," he countered. "We're going to take him back to the ranch where he grew up. That's where we'll give him a decent burial."

I was happy to hear Dad's words. On our way back to the house one or two dogs started to bark. Mom must have heard them and she came to the kitchen door.

"What happened? Didn't you bury Chopo at the *dompe*?" she asked curiously.

"No," I answered her. "We're going to bury him at the ranch."

"Is that right, *viejo* (dear)?" Mom asked, looking straight at Dad.

"That's right. We'll leave right after lunch. And we'll be back tomorrow because I have to go work on Monday."

We put Chopo in a gunny sack and loaded him in the car. By the time we got to the ranch it was late afternoon. Before Dad and I unloaded Chopo, I heard Mom's voice.

"Hijito, where do you wish to bury Chopo? Have you thought about it?"

"Yes I have, Mom. I want to bury him next to your chicken coop."

"And why the chicken coop?"

"Because Chopo always liked to chase your chickens! He got a kick out of seeing them fly in the air. He was happy teasing the chickens so I want him buried near a place that brought him happiness."

Mom smiled . . . and Dad nodded his head in agreement. Then he dug a deep trench. He didn't want the coyotes to disturb Chopo. While he dug, I saw Mom gathering a few rocks. After we buried Chopo, Mom placed them on top of the grave.

"Mom, what are the rocks for?"

"Hijito, they're to remind us that Chopo is buried there. May he rest in peace! Animals, like us humans, also surely have a special place in God's kingdom."

I looked at Mom. I felt at ease and happy.

El día que derramé una lágrima

EL NOMBRE DE MI querido perro era Chopo. Él fue el primero y el único perro que tuve de niño. Debido al modo doloroso y feo que murió nunca me dieron ganas de hablar de él hasta ahora.

Volvamos atrás el reloj. Yo tenía seis años cuando papá me regaló Chopo en el rancho en el Valle del Río Puerco en Nuevo México donde vivíamos yo y mi familia. De niño el tiempo es algo que yo tomaba por alto. Solamente me importaba cuando yo tenía hambre, me daba sueño, o se me interrumpía el tiempo jugando debido a tareas por hacer ya fueran del hogar o del rancho. Si no, el tiempo venía y desaparecía rutinariamente como las cuatro estaciones del año.

Hace más de setenta años desde que me hice el dueño orgulloso de Chopo, un bello perrito color beige y blanco. Llegó a ser mi fiel compañero durante tres años. Según fue creciendo, Chopo corría tras las gallinas de mamá de una manera juguetona. Era de carácter bondadoso. Yo lo quería mucho.

Al principio mamá lo dejaba dormir en el suelo de la recámara pero sólo porque era un perrito y las noches eran frías. Una vez que el clima calentaba, Chopo tenía que estarse fuera de la casa. Un día cuando menos pensé, mamá me plantó una pregunta.

—Hijito, ¿has pensado en algún nombre para tu perrito? No puedes estar llamándolo perrito. Tienes que bautizarlo—dijo mamá, y me hizo un guiño mamá.

—¿Como cuando bautizaron a mi hermanita en la iglesia?

—Bueno, no exactamente, pero debieras ponerle nombre. A los animales les gusta tener nombres lo mesmo que a nosotros los seres humanos. Por eso es que tu papá nombró a su caballo El Moro que quiere decir gris-azul.

Yo no tenía la menor idea qué nombre ponerle a mi perrito hasta una mañana antes del desayuno. Salté de la cama pero no podía encontrar mis chopos. No era la primera vez que yo los buscaba y buscaba. Por lo general hallaba a mi perrito jugando con ellos debajo de la cama. De buenas a primeras se me vino un nombre a la cabeza.

—¿A que no sabes qué, amá?—le dije todo emocionado mientras me acababa el aveno—. Le voy a poner el nombre Chopo a mi perrito.

—¿Por qué Chopo?—preguntó mamá.

—Porque cada vez que busco mis chopos, falta uno. Es por eso que quiero bautizarlo Chopo—y miré a mamá que se sonreía.

—Yo creo que es una idea ingeniosa y un buen nombre para tu perrito—añadió mamá—. Tu papá estará muy orgulloso de ti.

Esa tarde volvió papá de su trabajo. Mientras cenábamos, mamá rompió el silencio.

—Hijito, ¿que no le vas a dar a tu papá las buenas nuevas?

—¿Qué nuevas?—contesté un poco confuso.

—Ya tú sabes. Lo del perro.

—¡Oh sí!—dije tratando de poner en orden mis pensamientos—. Papá, tengo algo que decirte.

—¿De veras? ¿Y qué es eso?—preguntó antes de que yo pudiera continuar.

—Ahora tengo un nombre pa mi perrito. Desde hoy en adelante lo vamos a llamar Chopo.

—¡Chopo! ¿De dónde sacates un nombre como ése?—luego le di la misma explicación que le di a mi amá.

—Hijito, ése es un buen nombre. Me gusta. A los niños en nuestro barrio les gustará el nombre Chopo.

—¿Qué barrio?—exclamé yo en voz alta.

Las palabras de papá me pegaron como una buena patada en el estómago. Yo no sabía de qué hablaba. Mamá tampoco me había dicho que nos íbamos a mudar del rancho.

—Mijo—me dijo papá en un tono serio—, nos vamos ir del rancho y mudarnos a Alburquerque donde trataré de encontrar trabajo para mantener a la familia. Eso ya no es posible aquí en nuestro ranchito. En septiembre irás a una nueva escuela en la ciudá.

Nos mudamos al barrio de Santa Bárbara. Yo no estaba muy entusiasmado de ir a una nueva escuela. Empecé en la Escuela Elemental de Santa Bárbara. No quedaba muy lejos de la dispensa de mis abuelos paternales donde vivíamos ahora así que yo iba a pie. Ese primer día desayuné y luego salí a buscar a Chopo. Le grité. Estaba acostado debajo del carrito de papá.

—Chopo. Ven a comer. Tengo que irme a la escuela.

Ya para ahora sabía su nombre. Le di de comer y se comió todo en un decir amén.

—Bueno, ya me voy—y le acaricié la cabeza. Movió la cola; él estaba contento.

Entré en casa para despedirme de mamá. Cuando salí Chopo estaba en la puerta esperándome.

—Bueno, hasta la tarde amá.

Me di prisa porque no quería llegar tarde el primer día de clases. Cuando crucé Edith Boulevard al lado del cementerio Santa Bárbara un poco antes de llegar a la escuela, oí una voz.

—Oye perrito. ¿Tú vas a la escuela? ¿Qué te pasa? ¿Qué no hablas inglés?—dijo un muchachito que estaba rebotando un básquetbol camino a la escuela. Miré hacia atrás y vi a Chopo.

—Chopo, ¿qué haces aquí?

—¡Oye! ¿Cómo te llamas tú? ¿Y qué tu perro no habla inglés?—oí otra vez al muchacho pero lo ignoré—. Te pregunté algo. ¿Ése es tu perro?

—Sí—le respondí—. Él no te entiende. Solamente habla español.

—Pues, vale más que aprenda a hablar inglés como los perros en el barrio—me dijo de una manera amenazante. En ese momento se me acercó este muchacho.

—Cuida bien a tu perro—me advirtió—, porque por aquí hay perros muy malos.

—¿Y quién eres tú?—le pregunté.

—Yo soy Bobby Ortega. Yo vivo a dos puertas de tu agüela.

Agarré a Chopo del collar y lo llevé a casa tan pronto como pude. Mamá lo amarró en el garaje, y yo corrí a la escuela lo más recio posible. No quería llegar tarde.

La Escuela de Santa Bárbara tenía varios cuartos y maestras con diferentes niveles. Éste era un contraste con la escuela en el rancho de un cuarto y grados uno a ocho, y solamente una maestra.

Ese día los chicos en los terrenos de la escuela se burlaron de mis pantalones pecheras y de los zapatos altos. También se burlaron de la forma en que yo hablaba lo poco del inglés que sabía y cómo pronunciaba ciertas palabras con un acento español. Mis compañeros de clase no fueron muy cariñosos tampoco, pero aguanté como pude el primer día de escuela.

Cuando llegué a casa, Chopo estaba debajo del carrito de papá, su lugar favorito para descansar. Tan pronto como me vio, corrió hacia a mí.

—Epa, Chopo. ¿Qué tal?

Le acaricié la cabeza, y movió la cola. Estaba contentísimo de verme, y yo también estaba contento de verlo a él. Mamá oyó el ruido and salió de la cocina a saludarme.

—Hijito, ¡ya estás de vuelta! ¿Qué tal la escuela? A que te divertiste, ¿verdá?

—Güeno, sí y no—respondí sin mucho entusiasmo—. Esos escueleros atascaos se burlaron de mi inglés.

—No te amargues, hijito. Nada dura para siempre. Y acuérdate, 'En este mundo es mejor olvidar los insultos que recordar la venganza.'

—Bueno, amá—y allí dejé el asunto. No me atreví a decirle que los chicos se habían burlado de mis pantalones y los zapatos.

Me fue mejor el segundo día de escuela, y para el tercer día en vez de venir a casa para comer al mediodía, mamá me preparó huevos revueltos con papas fritas en una tortilla. Llevé en un paquete acafetado mi lonche y me lo comí en la cafetería donde muchos escueleros comían sus comidas calientes. Dos muchachos de mi clase me acompañaron, pero cuando vieron lo que comía, se rieron, hicieron un comentario sarcástico, y se fueron. Yo no le dije nada a mamá del incidente.

Al día siguiente ella me preparó calabacitas y maíz fritos envueltos en una tortilla, algo que siempre me había gustado mucho. Pero en vez de llevármelo a la escuela, se lo di a Chopo (sin que mamá supiera, claro) antes de irme. No quería que se burlaran otra vez los chicos de mi lonche.

No pasó nada sin incidentes el tercer día de escuela, pero para cuando llegué a casa, ya me moría de hambre. Mamá estaba sentada en su silla delante de la dispensa con mi hermanita Elsie en los brazos. Mamá se veía triste.

—Amá, ¿qué pasa?

—Hijito, ve mira a Chopo. Algo le pasa—dijo ella de una manera vaga.

—¿Qué? ¿Qué?—reaccioné muerto de miedo.

A primera vista creí que tal vez el culpable fuera mi sándwich de calabacitas y maíz, pero al acercarme a Chopo que estaba acostado debajo del carrito de papá, vi que tenía que ser algo mucho más serio. Me arrastré de estómago hacia él. No se movía. Pronto vi que tenía las orejas todas mordidas y ensangrentadas.

—Chopo, Chopo, ¿qué tienes? ¿Qué te pasó? ¿Quién hizo esto contigo?

Gemía y gemía. No me atreví a tocarle la cabeza, pero sí le acaricié la panza. La palma de la mano pronto se me empapó de la sangre que le escurría de las costillas. Me enfermé del estómago y comencé a llorar y a vomitarme. Mamá se puso de rodillas y vio lo desconsolado que estaba yo. Se metió debajo del carrito para consolarme.

—Amá, ¿qué le pasó a Chopo? ¿Sabes tú?—le pregunté creyendo que ella tal vez supiera.

—Hijito, Chopo por lo visto te siguió a la escuela pero en el camino lo atacó una perrada. Nuestro vecino don Melitón que vive al otro lado de la calle de nosotros oyó un bullicio en la calle. Trató de rescatar a Chopo de los perros, pero ya fue muy tarde. Chopo no sé cómo pudo andar a casa. Don Melitón lo siguió. Él fue el que me dijo de la perrada.

—Amá, ¿va a sanar Chopo o no?

—¿Quién sabe hijito? Todo está en manos de Dios.

Me dejó solo con Chopo. Lo miraba con mucho cuidado. Pronto vi que la panza se le movía cada vez más para arriba y para abajo. Yo le hablaba, pero parecía que tenía dificultad en respirar. Esto duró unos cuantos minutos. De pronto su cuerpo se sacudió y dejó de moverse. Le puse una oreja a la panza lo mismo que hizo mi abuelito en el rancho cuando murió su caballo. Chopo ya no respiraba. Mi querido perro se murió calladito ante mis ojos. Me sobrevino una tristeza profunda. Me sentí tan solo. Mi sentí vació por dentro. Me había perdido mi buen amigo. ¿Qué haría yo sin él?

Fui y le dije a mamá. No dejaba yo de llorar. Me abrazó y trató lo mejor posible de aliviar el dolor que yo sentía.

—Amá—le dije—, ojalá que nunca hubiéramos haber venido a este barrio. Ni siquiera los perros nos quieren. Yo quiero volver al rancho.

En ese dado momento llegó papá del trabajo y vio que yo estaba llorando.

—¿Qué pasa? ¿Pasa algo?—preguntó él con una cara de perplejo—. ¿Por qué sollozas?

—Se ha muerto Chopo—intercaló mamá—. Una perrada lo atacó ferozmente y lo mató. Anda mira tú mismo. Está debajo del carro.

—Apá, ¿qué vamos hacer ahora? ¿Qué vamos hacer con Chopo? No podemos dejarlo debajo del carro.

—Lo vamos a enterrar.

—¿Pero dónde?

—Mañana es sábado y no tengo que trabajar. Lo llevamos al basurero. Allí lo enterramos.

Esa noche no pude dormir del todo. Me di vueltas y vueltas toda la noche. No podía dejar de pensar en Chopo y lo mucho que lo iba a echar de menos. Después del desayuno, papá y yo echamos a Chopo en mi carrito colorado que me habían regalado él y mamá para la Navidad.

—Apá, ¿qué tan lejos está el basurero?

—No muy lejos. Tardamos poco tiempo en llegar. Está cerca del cementerio. ¿Ves ese humo más adelante? Es allí a dónde vamos.

Al caminar por el barrio, nos miraba la gente. Veían que llevábamos un perro muerto. Sin duda se preguntaban que si qué pasó, pero no estábamos con ganas de decirles aunque nos hubieran preguntado. Cuando llegamos al basurero, vi varias pilas de basura. Una de ella ardía a fuego lento. No era nada bonito. De pronto un hombre salió misteriosamente de detrás de la nube oscura de humo.

—¿En qué puedo servirle?—le preguntó a papá.

—El perro de mi hijo se murió y queremos enterrarlo.

—Lo siento. No enterramos animales muertos aquí—comentó de una manera fría y cruel—. Déjelo aquí y yo me encargo de él—añadió en una voz ronca.

Papá y yo descargamos a Chopo con mucho cuidado del carrito y lo pusimos en la tierra a un lado de unas cajas de cartón con el letrero *BIG HUNK CANDY*. Le di una palmadita a Chopo en la cabeza, me despedí de él, y me fui con lágrimas en los ojos.

—Un momentito—me dijo papá—. Vamos a echar a Chopo de nuevo en tu carrito. No lo vamos a dejar aquí en un montón de basura. Lo llevamos a casa.

Sus palabras me sorprendieron totalmente ya que casi nunca mostraba mucha emoción.

—Apá, ¿qué vamos hacer con Chopo? No hay lugar dónde enterrarlo en la yarda de mis abuelitos.

—No te apenes—respondió él—. Lo vamos a llevar al rancho donde se crio. Es allí donde le daremos un entierro decente.

Me dio gusto oír las palabras de papá. Camino a casa, uno o dos perros empezaron a ladrar. Mamá quizás los oyó y se acercó a la puerta de la cocina.

—¿Qué pasó? ¿Qué no enterraron a Chopo en el *dompe*?—preguntó ella con cierta curiosidad.

—No—le respondí yo—. Lo vamos a enterrar en el rancho.

—¿Es cierto, viejo?—preguntó mamá mirando directamente a papá.

—Es verdá. Nos marchamos poco después del lonche. Y regresamos mañana porque tengo que ir a trabajar el lunes.

Pusimos a Chopo en un saco de guangoche y lo echamos en el carrito de papá. Para cuando llegamos al rancho ya era por la tarde. Antes de que papá y yo bajáramos a Chopo, oí la voz de mamá.

—Hijito, ¿dónde quieres enterrar a Chopo? ¿Ya has pensando dónde?

—Sí, amá. Quiero enterralo cerca de tu gallinero.

—¿Y por qué el gallinero?

—¡Porque a Chopo siempre le gustaba correr tras tus gallinas! A él le encantaba verlas volar por el aire. Le daba gusto burlarse de las gallinas así que quiero enterralo cerca de un lugar que le trujo alegría.

Mamá se sonrió . . . y papá estuvo de acuerdo. Luego sacó él una zanja honda. No quería que los coyotes molestaran a Chopo. Mientras que papá escarbaba, vi que mamá recogía unas piedras. Después que enterramos a Chopo, mamá las puso encima del entierro.

—Amá, ¿para qué son las piedras?

—Hijito, son pa recordarnos que Chopo está enterrado aquí. ¡Que en paz descanse! Los animales igual que nosotros los seres humanos seguramente que tamién tienen un lugar especial en el reino de Dios.

Miré a mamá. Me sentí tranquilo y contento.

Chato the Woodchopper

AS USUAL, GRANDMA LALE had gone very early to Mass at San Ignacio Church with doña Francisquita, her next-door neighbor. That is something Grandma did at least twice a week including Sundays. The night before, she asked me to feed her chickens while she was at church.

Grandma Lale had a few chickens and a rooster in the chicken coop in a corner of her yard. That's where her eggs came from for breakfast and her other meals. In that way she didn't have to buy them at the store.

That morning, after I had eaten my oatmeal, Rainbo toast, and a slice of cantaloupe, I grabbed Grandma's five-pound can of corn that was in a corner of the chicken coop; it was covered with a lid. That way the mice that came out at night couldn't eat the corn. As soon as the chickens saw me they came to me. I quickly scattered corn on the ground. They cackled here and there, pecking at the corn. They were dying of hunger.

Upon leaving the chicken coop I saw this man who kept knocking at Grandma's kitchen door (it was customary to knock on neighbors' kitchen doors).

"Eh, eh, is yo, yo, gra', gra', 'ma, 'ma here?" he asked me, stuttering.

"No, she's at Mass," I responded, and he left with his head down and a bit dejected.

When my grandma returned, the first thing she asked me was if I had fed the chickens.

"Yes, yes," I answered hastily, "but I have something to tell you. This tall man wearing a cap who could barely talk, as if he was tongue-tied, stopped by. And not only that, he had an axe on his shoulder. I got really scared."

"Oh, hijito. Don't be afraid. That's Chato," she said, without much concern.

"And who is Chato? And why does he have such an ugly name? And not only that, he had one leg shorter than the other and he dragged it when he walked."

"All right, come in the kitchen. Sit down but listen carefully to what I say. His nickname is Chato because he was born with a pug nose. He's about twenty-eight or thirty years old, but the poor soul looks older. As you saw, he stutters. Do you understand what I'm saying?"

"Yes Grandma. I understand."

"But his parents love him very much. That's why they never sent him to school. They didn't want the kids to make fun of him. And poor Chato is even a little slow mentally, but as you will see, he's a good person. Is that clear, hijito?"

"Yes Grandma, but why was he carrying that axe? To defend himself if someone makes fun of him or what?"

"No, no, no. All the neighbors on our street and throughout the community know Chato and they love him very much. He uses the axe to chop wood for them. He goes from house to house and asks if they want him to chop wood for the cooking stove or their potbelly stove."

"And do they pay him or not, Grandma?"

"No doubt they give him a few cents so he can buy his *antojos*."

"And why does he need glasses? Chato seems to see fine without them."

"No, no, no. It has nothing to do with *anteojos*, glasses. It's *antojos*—cravings."

"And what are cra, cra . . . cravings?" I asked, having trouble saying the word.

"Cravings are when you really feel like eating something sweet. Do you understand?"

"Like when I get this strong desire to eat Mom's delicious *natillas* or Grandpa Lolo's chicharrones."

"That's it," Grandma said with a smile.

"Okay, I'm off. Mom is waiting for me."

As I left, I bumped into Chato at the door. He had returned.

"Eh, eh, is yur, yur gramma at 'ome?"

"Yes. She's inside washing dishes. I'll call her." I hollered at her. "Grandma! Chato is here," and she came to the door.

"Neighbor, I came to see if you wanted me to chop some wood for you," he said without stammering.

"Yes. There's a pile of thick logs. I want you to split those for me. And I also want you to clean the chicken coop. You know how," she said, and Chato nodded yes. "As you enter you'll see a bucket and a broom. When you're done come knock at the door. I'll be here."

It wasn't long before you heard the axe blows. Chato was strong and skilled with the axe. I was left with my mouth open.

"Okay, come. What's wrong? Why do you look so confused?" Grandma asked me.

"Why didn't Chato get tongue-tied when he spoke to you? When he spoke with me he got all choked up."

"Ah, that's easy to explain. When he doesn't know someone he gets nervous and tongue-tied. It doesn't matter if the person is young, old, woman, man, or child. Chato already knows me so his words don't get stuck in his throat. He speaks to me calmly, and with confidence. Do you understand what I'm saying?"

"Now I understand. Thank you Grandma."

I went to help Mom. She was washing dishes. I dried them and put them in the cupboard. After I had finished, Mom asked me to take Grandma a small jar of apricot jelly that Mom had just canned. Grandma was talking to Chato.

"Everything is wonderful! As always, you have done a good job. Here you are: fifteen cents for chopping the wood and ten cents for having cleaned the chicken coop."

"Thank you very much, neighbor. I'll see you next time," Chato said, and he left with a happy and shiny face.

He returned within a few minutes. I was pumping water from my grandma and grandpa's artesian well in front of their house.

"Do you want some?" he asked me, without stammering.

"What is it?"

"A popsicle."

"A what?" I said, without understanding that mysterious word.

"An orange-flavored popsicle," and he broke it in two parts and gave me half. "Now lick it, like this," he said, and he showed me how. "Do you like it?"

"Umm. I like it. The pop, pop . . . is very good. Now it's me whose words don't come out of my mouth," I said, and Chato smiled.

"Oh, by the *güey*," said Chato in English, which made me laugh because güey means stupid in Spanish, "what is your name?"

"My name is Junie, for Junior. That's what my family and friends call me. I'm Grandma Lale's grandson. By the way," I said, repeating his three words, "do you know English?" And he smiled.

"No. I heard those words from kids in the park. I don't even know what they mean. By the way," he repeated again with a smile, "would you like to go with me to ride the swings at school?"

"Yes, but I have to ask Mom's permission," I said, and Chato came with me.

"Mom, can I go with Chato to ride on the swings?"

"What swings?"

"At Santa Barbara School."

"Okay, but be careful. And don't stay long. I don't want to be worrying."

When we arrived there was nobody on the swings, but there were some boys nearby playing baseball. Chato got on one of the swings and I on another. He didn't take long in swinging way up high.

"Look at how high I can go up and down. I'm going to reach the clouds," he said in a loud voice that came and went as he was swinging.

Chato was happy as a child, but his joy did not last long. Two boys came close. Each one had a bottle of soda or something in their right hand. One was orange and the other was red. They knew who Chato was.

"Heh, heh, hey Cha, Cha, Chato," said one of them, mimicking Chato in a loud voice. "Would you like a sip of my Cu, cu, cu, Culo (pussy) Aid? It's very tasty."

"Let's go, Chato. Let's go quickly," I repeated.

"Come drink from my Culo Aid that's fresh and really sweet like my sweetheart's *culo*," added his partner.

"Let's go, Chato. I don't like what I hear," and we went back to my house. Then he left for his. We both lived on Wilson Avenue. (Currently it's Aspen Avenue.)

"How did you do at the swings, hijito?"

"Okay."

"Is that all you have to say? That face of yours that I know so well doesn't lie to me. Come, tell me. What happened?"

"Mom, some boys made fun of Chato. And they used an ugly word in Spanish and one in English that I didn't understand."

"Listen, hijito. On this earth there are good and mean people. But God looks after innocent souls like Chato. Moreover, he has a good heart."

"Is that why he gave me part of his popsicle?"

"Yes. And remember that everything good from people like Chato comes from the heart," said Mom touching her chest.

"Okay, Mom," and I gave her a hug.

"Here. Drink this lemonade that I just made."

"Is it sweet Mom?"

“Ah, funny you should ask, dear son. It can be sweet or sour just like people on this earth who are either good or mean-spirited. There you have don Hilario, who is nice.”

“And who is don Hilario, Mom?”

“You’ll see. One of these days your Grandma Lale will tell you. She knows him well.”

Chato el partidor de leña

COMO DE COSTUMBRE ABUELITA Lale se había ido muy temprano a misa en la iglesia de San Ignacio con doña Francisquita, su vecina de al lado. Esto es algo que mi abuelita hacía por lo menos dos veces por semana incluso los domingos. La noche anterior me pidió que les echara de comer a sus gallinas mientras ella estaba en misa.

Mi abuelita Lale tenía unas cuantas gallinas y un gallo en el gallinero en un rincón de su yarda. De allí le venían los huevos para el desayuno y sus otras comidas. Así no tenía que comprarlos en la tienda.

Esa mañana después que desayuné el aveno, pan tostado Rainbo, y una rebanada de melón roñoso, agarré un bote de cinco libras que tenía mi abuelita en un rincón del gallinero. Estaba cubierto con una tapadera. Así los ratoncitos que salían de noche no podían comerse el maíz. Tan pronto como me vieron las gallinas se me vinieron encima. No tardé en desparramarles maíz en la tierra. Cacareaban por aquí y por allá pepenando maíz. Estaban que se morían de hambre.

Al salir del gallinero vi a este hombre que estaba toque y toque en la puerta de la cocina de mi abuelita (era costumbre tocar la puerta de la cocina de vecinos).

—¿Eh, eh, está tu, tu, 'bue, bue, lita?—me preguntó tartamudeando.

—No, está en misa—le contesté, y se fue con la cabeza agachada y un poco desconsolado.

Cuando regresó mi abuelita, lo primero que me preguntó fue que si les había dado de comer a las gallinas.

—Sí, sí—le contesté rápidamente—pero tengo algo que decirle—. Estuvo aquí este hombre alto con cachucha que apenas podía hablar, como que se le trababa la lengua. Y no sólo eso, traiba una hacha en el hombro. Me dio muncho miedo.

—Oh, hijito. No tengas miedo. Es Chato—dijo ella sin mucha preocupación.

—¿Y quién es Chato? ¿Y por qué tiene ese nombre tan feo? Y no solamente eso, tenía una pierna más corta que la otra y la arrastraba cuando andaba.

—Güeno, vente a la cocina. Siéntate pero escucha bien lo que te digo. Su sobrenombre es Chato porque nació con la nariz chata. Él tiene unos veinte y ocho o treinta años, pero el pobrecito se ve más viejo. Como has visto, tartamudea. ¿Comprendes lo que te digo?

—Sí, agüelita. Comprendo.

—Pero sus padres lo quieren mucho. Por eso nunca lo enviaron a la escuela. No querían que se burlaran los estudiantes de él. Y el pobre Chato hasta está un poco atrasado de la mente, pero como ya verás, él es una buena persona. ¿Está claro eso, hijito?

—Sí, agüelita, ¿pero por qué traiba esa hacha? ¿Pa defenderse si alguien se burla de él o qué?

—No, no, no. Todos los vecinos en nuestra calle y por toda la vecindá conocen a Chato y lo quieren mucho. Usa l'hacha pa partirles leña. Él va de casa en casa y pregunta si quieren que les parta leña pa la estufa o el fogón.

—¿Y le pagan agüelita, o no?

—Seguro que le dan sus centavitos pa que compre sus antojos.

—¿Y por qué necesita anteojos? Chato parece que ve bien sin ellos.

—No, no, no. No tiene naa que ver con anteojos. Es antojos.

—¿Y qué son an, an . . . antojos?—pregunté batallando con la palabra.

—Antojos es como cuando le dan a uno muchas ganas de comer algo dulce. ¿Comprendes?

—Como cuando me dan ganas de comer las sabrosas natillas de mi amá o los chicharrones de Agüelito Lolo.

—Eso es—dijo mi agüelita con una sonrisa.

—Güeno, ya me voy. Mi amá me está esperando.

Al salir me topé con Chato en la puerta. Había vuelto de nuevo.

—¿Eh, eh, 'sta tu, tu 'buela en casa?

—Sí. Está dentro lavando trastes. Ya la llamo—y le grité—. ¡Agüelita! Aquí está Chato—y vino ella a la puerta.

—Vecina, vine a ver si quería que le partiera leña—dijo él sin trabársele la lengua.

—Sí. Ahi tengo una pila de troncos gruesos. Quiero que me los rajes. Y tamién quiero que me limpies el gallinero. Ya sabes cómo—y Chato movió la cabeza que sí—. Al entrar verás una cubeta y una escoba. Cuando acabes, ven y toca la puerta. Aquí voy a estar.

No tardó en oírse los hachazos. Chato era fuerte y diestro con el hacha. Yo me quedé con la boca abierta.

—Güeno, ven. ¿Qué te pasa? ¿Por qué te ves tan confuso?—me preguntó mi agüelita.

—¿Por qué a Chato no se le trabó la lengua cuando le habló a usté? Cuando habló conmigo se le atarugaron las palabras.

—Ah, eso es fácil de explicar. Cuando no conoce a alguien se pone nervioso y se la traba la lengua. No importa si la persona es joven, mayor, mujer, hombre o un niño. A mí ya me conoce Chato de manera que no se le atoran las palabras. Él me habla con calma y con toda confianza. ¿Me entiendes lo que te digo?

—Ahora sí comprendo. Gracias agüelita.

Me fui a ayudarle a mamá. Ella estaba lavando trastes. Yo los secaba y los ponía en el trastero. Al terminar me pidió mamá que le llevara a mi abuelita un frasquito de jalea de albaricoque que mamá acababa empacar. Mi abuelita estaba hablando con Chato.

—¡Qué bonito quedó todo! Como siempre, haz hecho buen trabajo. Aquí tienes: quince centavos por partir la leña, y diez por haber limpiado el gallinero.

—Muchas gracias, vecina. Ya nos vemos la próxima vez—dijo Chato y se despidió con una cara alegre y relumbrante.

Retornó dentro de unos minutos. Yo estaba pompeando agua de la noria de mis abuelitos en frente de su casa.

—¿Quieres?—me preguntó él sin tartamudear.

—¿Qué es?

—Un *popsicle*.

—¿Un qué?—dije sin entender aquella palabra misteriosa.

—Un popsicle de naranja—y lo quebró en dos partes y me dio la mitad—. Ora lámbelo, asina como yo—y me enseñó cómo—. ¿Te gusta?

—Umm. Me gusta. El pop, pop . . . está muy suave. Ahora soy yo a quien no le salen las palabras de la boca—y se sonrió Chato.

—Oh, *by the güey,*—dijo Chato en inglés, lo cual me hizo reír porque güey quiere decir estúpido en español—. ¿Cómo te llamas tú?

—Yo me llamo Junie por Junior. Asina me llaman mi familia y mis amigos. Soy nieto de mi agüelita Lale. *By the way,*—dije repitiendo sus tres palabras—. ¿Tú sabes inglés?—y él se sonrió.

—No. Yo oí esas palabras de la plebe en el parque. Ni siquiera sé qué quieren decir. *By the güey*—volvió a repetir con una sonrisa—, ¿quieres ir conmigo a pasearte en los columpios de la escuela?

—Sí, pero tengo que pedirle permiso a mi amá—y se vino Chato conmigo—. Amá, ¿puedo ir con Chato a pasearme en los columpios?

—¿Qué columpios?

—En la escuela de Santa Bárbara.

—Güeno, pero ten cuidao. Y no te estés largo rato. No quiero estar con la pena.

Cuando llegamos no había nadie en los columpios, pero sí

estaban unos muchachos cerca jugando al béisbol. Se subió Chato en un columpio y yo en otro. No tardó en columpiarse bien alto él.

—Mira lo alto que subo parriba y pabajo. Voy a llegar hasta las nubes—dijo en voz alta que iba y venía según se columpiaba.

Chato estaba contento como un niño, pero su alegría duró poco. Se acercaron dos muchachos. Cada uno traía una botella de soda o algo en la mano derecha. Una era color de naranja y la otra colorada. Ellos sabían quién era Chato.

—O, o, o, órale Cha, Cha, Chato—dijo uno de ellos en voz alta remedando a Chato—. ¿Quieres un trago de mi Cu, cu, cu, Culo Aid? Está muy sabroso.

—Ámonos, Chato. Amos pronto—le repetí.

—Ven bebe de mi Culo Aid que está fresco y muy dulce como el culo de mi güisa—añadió su compañero.

—Ámonos, Chato. No me gusta lo que oigo—y volvimos a mi casa. Luego se fue él a la suya. Ambos vivíamos en la calle Wilson. (Hoy día es Aspen.)

—¿Cómo te jue en los columpios, hijito?

—Bien.

—¿Es todo lo que tienes que decir? Esa cara tuya que conozco tan bien no me miente. Ven, dime. ¿Qué pasó?

—Amá. Unos muchachos se burlaron de Chato. Y usaron una palabra en español muy fea y otra en inglés que yo no entendí.

—Mira hijito. En este mundo hay gentes buenas y malas. Pero Dios cuida a los inocentes como Chato. Además, él es una persona de buen corazón.

—¿Es por eso que él me dio parte de su popsicle?

—Sí. Y acuérdate que todo lo bueno de personas como Chato viene del corazón—dijo mamá palpándose el pecho.

—Güeno, amá—y le di un abrazo.

—Toma. Bébete esta limonada que acabo de hacer.

—¿Está dulce amá?

—Ah, cosa curiosa que me preguntes hijito. Puede ser dulce o amarga tal como la gente en este mundo que es buena o de mal corazón. Ahi tienes a don Hilario que es buena gente.

—¿Y quién es don Hilario, amá?

—Ya verás. Uno de estos días te dirá tu agüelita Lale. Ella lo conoce bien.

Don Hilario and His Hogs

WE WERE SMACK IN the middle of summer. My little brother Beltrán and I spent the night in Dad's car. He slept in the front seat under the steering wheel, and I in the back. That way I wasn't stooped on my knees all night long. Not only that, if both of us slept in the car the family wasn't as crowded in the small room where seven of us family members lived.

That night like many other nights, I couldn't sleep from the heat. What's more, my little brother wouldn't stop snoring until I woke up early in the morning. The breaking of dawn near the Santa Barbara Cemetery was barely upon us. I lowered the car's window on my side to get a little fresh air. As I opened it a whiff of a really foul odor hit me. "I wonder what it is," I said to myself.

Mom always got up early to fix Dad's breakfast before he went to work at Crane O'Fallon Company. I saw that she was awake because you could see the light coming from the kerosene lantern. I went to greet her a good morning. She was frying eggs.

"Hijito, what are you doing up so early? Look at you. You haven't even wiped the matter from your eyes. Did you sleep okay or not?"

"No, Mom. Beltrán snored all night long like a frog. And do you know something else?"

"What, hijito?"

"As I woke up I opened the car window and a whiff of a foul odor hit me."

"It probably comes from the outhouse or who knows where. Go ask your grandma. She surely knows."

"Good Morning, Grandma Lale. How are you this morning?"

"All right. But what are you doing up so early?"

"I came to ask you something. What is that odor I smell?"

"Oh, it comes from don Hilario's hogs, our neighbor from across the back alley, *callejón*. (Today it bears the name Martínez Avenue). He has about six or seven hogs, at times even more. When they are grown he sells them. That's how he earns a living. Come with me so you can meet him."

We went out the gate that faced the alley. Don Hilario's house was nearby. The closer we got, the stronger the smell. I covered my nose. My grandma knocked on the door that faced the patio.

"Good morning, neighbor."

"Good morning, *comadre*."

"I came for you to meet my grandson. His name is Junie García. He just moved from the ranch with his parents, Nasario and Agapita. He wants to see your pigs," Grandma said, and she winked at me.

"Good morning, young man. Come. There they are all together, except for the female pig and her piglets. They were born recently and I have them separated with the mother."

By now the odor coming from the pigpen with the larger hogs seemed to have disappeared.

"Today is Wednesday," explained don Hilario, "and in a little bit I'm leaving to see what leftovers I can find in the neighborhood for my pigs. There's my buggy and Sancho, my horse. They're waiting for me. You want to come with me, young man?"

"Thanks, neighbor. Perhaps some other time," interjected my grandma, and we returned home.

It didn't take long before you could hear Sancho trotting down the alley and the loud clatter of the two lead barrels bouncing up and down in the carriage. Don Hilario visited merchants at least three times per week—Mondays, Wednesdays, and Fridays—to look for scraps. From time to time he even went on Saturdays if there was some kind of a fiesta in the community.

The first stop was El Porvenir Bar and the second one, Rodarte's Bar. The two were located on Edith Boulevard near the San Ignacio Church, north of Mountain Road, about a mile from don Hilario's house. There he picked up scraps for his hogs. As he returned home he stopped at Santa Barbara School and at Tom's Grocery Store, both on Edith Boulevard. The latter was next to the school. His last stop ordinarily was the Felipe García Store. As don Hilario reached home, the hogs evidently heard Sancho's trots and the noise coming from the buggy because they started grunting and grunting.

Don Hilario was an elderly bachelor, about sixty-five or seventy years old. As a young man it is said that he had his share of girlfriends, but not one reached the doorstep of his liking and well-being. Now he devoted his entire life to his pigs, which he sold to purchase food for himself and a shirt here and there or a pair of pants and shoes. With part of the money he also bought corn and wheat to fatten the hogs.

But don Hilario was a generous man. Every autumn, whether in October or November, when it wasn't as hot, he hosted a Matanza. He invited his neighbors who lived nearby including my grandma.

One Saturday morning I heard banging on the screen door to our little house.

"Come, go see who it is, hijito," said Mom, and I saw that it was my grandma.

"Good morning. Would you like to come with me to see don Hilario?"

"And what are we going to do there, Grandma?"

"I can't tell you," she said with a wry smile. "It's a surprise."

"Mom, can I go with Grandma Lale to visit don Hilario?"

"Go! Enjoy yourself," Mom said without hesitation.

Grandma grabbed me by the hand and we headed for the alley. We went directly to don Hilario's patio, which was quite large. The first thing I saw was a bunch of men chatting around a bonfire.

Long flames shot into the heavens. To one side of the fire there was a large wooden table. A little beyond, one could see a group of women kneading dough and making tortillas.

It wasn't long before you heard noises. A burst of shouts and applause erupted. Six burly men were carrying a hog in their arms. Upon seeing the scene, I tugged at one of Grandma's hands.

"Grandma! Grandma! This is like Grandpa Lolo's Matanza at the ranch," I said, all excited.

"Yes and no. Here the majority of adults and children don't see how a hog is killed. One more thing, don Hilario and his friends have already scraped the pig's bristle before they came out to the patio."

"And what's going to happen now, Grandma?" I asked, even though I had seen two or three of Grandpa's Matanzas before we moved to Albuquerque.

"Ah, your question is music to my ears. Now comes the good part—the crispy *chicharrones* (pork rinds)!"

The words had barely left Grandma's mouth when a woman put a hot tortilla in my hands.

"Come, young man. Get close to the fire so they can put chicharrones in your tortilla. For a good appetite there's nothing better than really hot chicharrones."

I stood behind some kids who were waiting their turn. Don Hilario and two of his *compadres*, Melitón and Bernabé, tended to the fire and were frying chicharrones in a large cauldron. He recognized me, stuck his big ladle in the pan, and put a few chicharrones on my flour tortilla. I folded it and took the first bite. Tasty like Grandpa Lolo's.

In the meantime I saw a few elderly women seated at a wooden table preparing the ingredients for blood sausages. Each one would take home a *morcilla* to cook. The men themselves, with knives and saws, had begun to quarter the hog to share it among the neighbors. The women, with pans in their hands, awaited their small portion of meat. Such a gesture was typical of don Hilario every time he celebrated a Matanza. He gave away the entire hog except for the head.

He kept it because he knew that the meat from the hog's head was the best part to make tamales at Christmastime. Grandma Lale did something similar at the ranch.

In midafternoon, one by one the neighbors thanked don Hilario before they left for their homes. My grandma and I also thanked him and returned home. She was carrying her small piece of meat, and I, my small jar of chicharrones.

As all the people departed, don Hilario sat on the porch that faced the patio where the Matanza had been enjoyed. All of a sudden an inexhaustible silence overcame him. The bonfire, whose ashes scarcely sparkled, made faint noises. He grabbed a bucket of water and tossed it on the few ashes that still glowed. Next he went to the table where the forlorn pig's head rested. He caressed it and then carried the head delicately in his arms and took it to his storage shed, where it was cool. There he hung the head from a beam. Now it was time to wait until Christmastime when he would make his tamales.

Don Hilario continued his trips week after week to collect leftovers from the merchants to feed his hogs. A few days after Thanksgiving, Paloma, who lived next door to don Hilario, realized that he hadn't been around. She became worried. She went and knocked on the kitchen door, but there was no answer. She entered and found him seated in a rocking chair with his head down, as though he were resting or asleep.

"Neighbor, neighbor!" she uttered softly, "are you all right? Are you all right or not? It's me—Paloma," but there was no response. She shook him gently by the shoulders, and his body fell to the floor.

Paloma was startled and took off running. I was chopping wood when I saw her enter through the gate to the alley to tell my grandma.

"Neighbor, neighbor! Something has happened to don Hilario,"

Paloma uttered, barely catching her breath. "I shook him, but he doesn't respond. He doesn't move. Nothing. Come, come quickly!" The two left in a hurry. I followed them.

They took his pulse, first on the left wrist, and then the right one, but there were no signs of life. At that instant don Bernabé came in. He had seen my grandma and Paloma running.

"What's wrong, neighbors? What's wrong?" And he saw that don Hilario was flat on the floor and wasn't moving. His eyes were droopy. He was dead.

Since don Hilario was a fairly large man, don Bernabé, my grandma, and Paloma lifted him with great difficulty and put him in his bed. In the evening the priest from the San Ignacio Church came and gave him the last rites.

It wasn't long before the neighborhood found out that don Hilario had died. That same evening a rosary was said at his home. The body lay in state in front of a small altar that Paloma had improvised. Numerous people went to pay their respects.

The following day don Bernabé and his compadres placed the body in a modest wooden coffin that the local carpenter had built. After hitching Sancho to don Hilario's horse buggy that he used in his rounds week after week in search of something to eat for his hogs, they loaded the coffin onto the buggy and headed for the San Ignacio Church to celebrate Mass. Walking behind them was a shiny red hog—don Hilario's favorite—and the mourners. The priest was at the end of the procession.

Following Mass, attended by a myriad of people including some merchants, the deceased was taken to the Santa Barbara Cemetery for burial. Six men unloaded the coffin from the horse carriage and placed it alongside the grave. Thereafter three of them on either side, using strong horsehair ropes, carefully lowered the coffin into the grave.

The priest said a brief prayer and offered his blessings. A handful of men, with hat in hand, made the sign of the cross while the women offered their prayers.

One by one the neighbors grabbed a fistful of dirt and tossed it gently on top of the coffin. A man who was to one side of me whispered, "Good-bye my friend. May God rest your soul," and he left, crestfallen. My grandma told me that the man had been a friend of don Hilario back in Cubero where the two had grown up together.

On the way back to don Hilario's home, don Bernabé did not climb back onto the buggy but rather grabbed Sancho's reins and walked in front. As he went inside the yard a silence came over him. Not even the hogs made a noise. Perhaps they themselves sensed that the man who had once fed them had left for another world.

With the demise of don Hilario the Matanza that took place yearly ended a long-standing tradition that he had brought to Santa Barbara years back from Cubero.

A few days after the death of her beloved neighbor, Paloma, out of sheer curiosity, entered his storage shed. The first thing she saw was the hog's head. Pinned to one of its ears—and much to her astonishment—was a small piece of paper with the words in capital letters that read, PARA TI PALOMA. LA NAVIDAD Y LOS TAMALES TE AGUARDAN (FOR YOU, PALOMA. CHRISTMAS AND TAMALES AWAIT YOU).

Don Hilario y sus marranos

ESTÁBAMOS EN PLENO VERANO. Mi hermanito Beltrán y yo pasamos la noche en el carro de papá. Él durmió bajo el volante en el asiento de adelante, y yo en el de atrás. De ese modo no estaba yo encogido de rodillas toda la noche. No solamente eso, si dormíamos los dos en el carro así la familia no estaba tan amontonada en el cuartito donde vivíamos siete de familia.

Esa noche como muchas otras noches no pude dormir del calor que hacía. Además, mi hermanito no dejaba de roncar hasta que despertaba yo temprano por la mañana. Apenas venía rayando el sol al levante cerca del cementerio de Santa Bárbara. Bajé la ventana a mi lado del carro para que entrara un fresquecito. Al abrirla me pegó un tufo pero feo. "¿Qué será?" Me pregunté.

Mamá siempre se levantaba temprano para prepararle desayuno a papá antes que se fuera a trabajar en Crane O'Fallon Company. Vi que ya estaba despierta porque se veía la luz de la lámpara de aceite. Fui a darle los buenos días. Ella estaba friendo huevos.

—Hijito, ¿qué haces tan de mañana? Mira nomás. Ni siquiera te has limpiado las lagañas. ¿Dormites bien o no?

—No, amá. Beltrán roncó la noche entera como una rana. ¿Y sabes qué, amá?

—¿Qué hijito?

—Al recordar abrí la ventana del carro y me pegó un tufo murre feo.

—Seguro que viene del escusao o quién sabe de dónde. Ve pregúntale a tu agüela. Ella debe saber.

—Buenos días, Lale. ¿Cómo amaneció?

—Bien. ¿Pero qué haces tú tan tempranito?

—Vine a preguntarle algo. ¿Qué es ese tufo que huelo?

—Oh, viene de los marranos del vecino don Hilario al otro lado del callejón (Hoy día lleva por nombre Martínez Avenue). Él tiene unos seis o siete, a veces hasta más. Cuando ya crecen los vende. Asina es cómo se mantiene él. Vamos conmigo pa que lo conozcas.

Salimos por la puerta que daba al callejón. La casa de don Hilario quedaba cerquita. Mientras más nos fuimos acercando, más fuerte el apeste. Me tapé la nariz. Tocó mi abuelita la puerta que daba al patio.

—Buenos días, vecino.

—Buenos días, comadre.

—Vine pa que conozca a mi nieto. Se llama Junie. Acaba de mudarse del rancho con sus padres Nasario y Agapita. Él quiere ver sus marranos—dijo mi abuelita, y me hizo un guiño ella.

—Buenos días joven. Ven. Ahi están todos juntos menos la marrana y sus marranitos. Ellos nacieron hace poco y los tengo aparte con la mamá.

Ya para ahora parecía haber desaparecido el tufo que venía del trochil donde estaban los marranos grandes.

—Hoy es miércoles— explicó don Hilario—, y dentro de poco salgo a ver qué sobras hallo por la vecindá pa mis cochinos. Ahi tengo mi boguecito y Sancho, mi caballo. Ya me esperan. ¿Quieres ir conmigo joven?

—Gracias vecino. Tal vez en otra ocasión—interrumpió mi abuelita, y volvimos a casa.

No tardó mucho en oírse por el callejón el trote de Sancho y el estrépito de los dos barriles vacíos de estaños que saltaban en el bogue. Don Hilario visitaba a comerciantes por lo general tres veces por semana, los lunes, miércoles, y viernes, en busca de sobras. De vez en cuando hasta salía los sábados si había alguna fiesta en la comunidad.

La primera parada era la cantina El Porvenir y la segunda el Bar Rodarte. Las dos quedaban en Edith Boulevard cerca de la Iglesia de San Ignacio al norte de Mountain Road como a una milla de la casa de don Hilario. Allí recogía sobras de comida para sus marranos. Al regresar a casa paraba en la escuela de Santa Bárbara y en la Tom's Grocery, ambas en Edith Boulevard. Ésta quedaba al lado de la escuela. Su última parada solía ser el comercio de Felipe García. Al llegar don Hilario a casa quizás los marranos oyeron el trote de Sancho y el ruido del bogue porque allí estaban gruñe que gruñe.

Don Hilario era solterón con sus sesenta y cinco o setenta años de edad. De joven se dice que tuvo sus novias, pero ninguna de ellas llegó a la puerta de su gusto y bien estar. Ahora dedicaba su vida entera a sus marranos los cuales vendía para comprarse comida y una que otra camisa o un par de pantalones y zapatos. Con parte del dinero también compraba maíz y trigo para engordar los cochinos.

Pero don Hilario era un hombre generoso. Cada otoño ya fuera en octubre o noviembre cuando no hacía tanto calor, él celebraba una matanza. Invitaba a sus vecinos que vivían cerca, incluso a mi abuelita.

Un sábado por la mañana oí unos toques en la puerta de alambre de nuestra casita.

—Anda, mira a ver quién es hijito—me pidió mamá, y vi que era mi abuelita.

—Buenos días. ¿Quieres ir conmigo a ver a don Hilario?

—¿Y qué vamos hacer allá, agüelita?

—No te puedo decir—me dijo con una risita—. Es una sorpresa.

—Amá, ¿puedo ir con mi agüelita Lale a visitar a don Hilario?

—¡Ve! Diviértete—dijo mama sin dudarlo.

Me agarró de la mano mi abuelita y salimos al callejón. Nos fuimos derecho al patio de don Hilario que era bastante grande. Lo primero que vi fue un puño de hombres platicando alrededor de una hoguera que escupía largas llamas hacia el cielo. A un lado de la lumbre estaba una mesa grande de madera. Un poco más allá se veían unas mujeres amasando y echando tortillas.

No tardó en oírse unos ruidos. Rompieron gritos y aplausos. Se vieron seis hombres garrudos que venían con un marrano en los brazos. Al ver aquella escena, le jalé una mano a mi abuelita.

—¡Agüelita, agüelita! Esto es como la matanza de mi abuelito Lolo en el rancho—le dije todo emocionado.

—Casi sí y casi no. Aquí en Santa Bárbara la mayoría de los mayores y los niños no ven cómo se mata un marrano. Otra cosa, don Hilario y sus amigos ya lo han pelado antes de entrar con él en el patio.

—¿Y qué va pasar ahora agüelita?—, aunque yo había visto dos o tres matanzas de Abuelito Lolo antes de mudarnos a Alburquerque.

—Ah, tu pregunta es música para mis oídos. Ahora viene lo bueno. ¡Los chicharrones!

No acababan de escapársele las palabras a mi abuelita cuando me puso una señora una tortilla calentita en las manos.

—Anda, jovencito. Arrímate a la lumbre pa que te pongan chicharrones en tu tortilla. Pa un güen hambre no hay como chicharrones calientitos.

Me puse detrás de otros niños que esperaban su turno. Don Hilario y dos de sus compadres, Melitón y Bernabé, atizaban la lumbre y freían chicharrones en un calderón grande. Don Hilario me reconoció, metió su cucharón en la olla, y me puso unos cuantos chicharrones en la tortilla. La doblé y tomé el primer bocado. Sabrosos como los de mi abuelito Lolo.

Mientras tanto vi sentadas unas ancianas en una mesita de madera preparando los ingredientes para morcillas. Cada una se llevaría su morcilla a casa para cocinarla. Los hombres mismos con cuchillos y serruches habían empezado a descuartizar el marrano para repartirlo entre los vecinos. Las mujeres con bandejas en las manos esperaban su regalito de carne. Tal gesto era típico de don

Hilario cada vez que celebraba una matanza. Él regalaba todo el cochino menos la cabeza.

Él se quedaba con ella porque sabía que la carne de la cabeza del marrano era lo mejor para hacer tamales durante la Navidad. Cosa igual hacía mi abuelita Lale en el rancho.

A mediados de la tarde los vecinos uno por uno le dieron las gracias a don Hilario antes de volver a sus hogares. Yo y mi abuelita también le dimos las gracias y regresamos a casa. Ella llevaba su trocito de carne, y yo mi frasquito de chicharrones.

Al despedirse toda la gente, se sentó don Hilario en el portal que daba al patio donde se celebró la matanza. De buenas a primeras le sobrevino un silencio inagotable. La hoguera cuyas brasas chispeaban apenas hacían unos ruiditos. Agarró él una cubeta con agua y se la echó a las pocas brazas que todavía ardían. Luego se acercó a la mesa donde estaba solita la cabeza del marrano. La acarició y después la cogió delicadamente en brazos y se la llevó a su despensa donde estaba fresco. Allí colgó la cabeza de una viga. Ahora había que esperar hasta la Navidad cuando haría sus tamales.

Don Hilario continuaba sus viajes semana tras semana para recoger sobras de los mercantes para sus marranos. Unos días después del Día de Gracias, se dio cuenta Paloma, vecina que vivía al lado de don Hilario, que no se había visto él. Le dio pena a Paloma. Fue y toco en la puerta de la cocina, pero no hubo respuesta. Entró y allí lo halló sentado en una silla mecedora con la cabeza agachada como que estaba descansando o dormido.

—¡Vecino, vecino!—le habló ella calladitamente—. ¿Está bien? ¿Está bien o no? Soy yo Paloma—, pero no hubo respuesta. Lo sacudió con cuidado de los hombres, y el cuerpo fue a dar al suelo.

Paloma se espantó y salió corriendo. Yo estaba partiendo leña cuando la vi entrar por la puerta del callejón a avisarla a mi abuelita.

—¡Vecina, vecina! Algo le ha pasado a don Hilario—dijo Paloma apenas sin resuello—. Lo sacudí, pero no responde. No se mueve. Nada. ¡Venga, venga pronto!—y salieron las dos de prisa. Yo las seguí.

Le tomaron el pulso, primero en la muñeca izquierda, y luego en la derecha, pero no hubo señas de vida. En eso entró don Bernabé, vecino y amigo de don Hilario que vio a Paloma y a mi abuelita correr.

—¿Qué pasa vecinas? ¿Qué pasa?—y vio que don Hilario estaba estirado en el suelo y que no se movía. Tenía los ojos clisados. Estaba muerto.

Como don Hilario era un hombre bastante grande, lo levantaron a duras penas don Bernabé, mi abuelita, y Paloma y lo acostaron en su cama. Por la tarde vino el cura de la Iglesia de San Ignacio y le otorgó los últimos sacramentos.

No tardó la vecindad en saber que don Hilario había fallecido. Esa misma tardecita se celebró un rosario en su casa. El cuerpo fue velado delante de un pequeño altar que había improvisado Paloma. Fue mucha gente a expresar sus respetos.

Al día siguiente don Bernabé y sus compadres colocaron el cuerpo en un cajón sencillo de madera que había hecho el carpintero de la vecindad. Tras prender a Sancho del bogue de don Hilario que usaba en sus recorridos semana tras semana en busca de algo que comer para sus marranos, cargaron el cajón en el bogue y se dirigieron a la Iglesia de San Ignacio para celebrar misa. Detrás de ellos iba un cochino colorado relumbroso—el favorito de don Hilario—y los dolientes. El cura iba al final de la procesión.

Después de la misa, donde hubo un sinfín de gente, incluso algunos comerciantes, llevaron al difunto al Campo Santo de Santa Bárbara para sepultarlo. Seis hombres bajaron el cajón del bogue y lo colocaron a un lado de la sepultura. Luego tres de ellos en cada lado con unos cabestros fuertes bajaron el cajón con mucho cuidado en el sepulcro.

El cura rezó una pequeña oración y echó la bendición. Los hombres respetuosamente con sombrero en la mano se persignaron mientras que las mujeres ofrecieron sus oraciones.

Uno que otro vecino cogió un puño de tierra y lo echaron suavemente sobre el cajón. Un hombre que estaba a mi lado murmuró,

"Adiós amigo. Que Dios te guarde en tu santa Gloria," y se despidió cabizbajo. Mi abuelita me dijo que el hombre fue amigo de don Hilario en Cubero donde se criaron juntos los dos.

Para regresar a casa de don Hilario, don Bernabé no se subió en el bogue sino que agarró a Sancho de las riendas y se fue andando a pie por delante hasta llegar al hogar de don Hilario. Al entrar en la yarda le sobrevino un silencio. Ni los marranos hacían ruido. Quizás ellos mismos sintieron que el hombre que les daba de comer ya se había ido a otro mundo.

Con la muerte de don Hilario la matanza que se llevaba a cabo una vez al año dio por fin a una larga tradición que él trajo a Santa Bárbara años atrás desde Cubero.

Unos días después de la muerte de su querido vecino, Paloma por pura curiosidad entró en la despensa. Lo primero que vio fue la cabeza del marrano. Prendido en una oreja con un alfiler—lo cual la sorprendió mucho—estaba un pequeño papel en letra mayúscula que decía, PARA TI PALOMA. LA NAVIDAD Y LOS TAMALES TE AGUARDAN.

Wanna Go to the Movies?

LITTLE BY LITTLE I met young people like Paloma and kids my age who lived nearby or on the same street as me. Two of them were Pat Perea and Danny Seiler, whose father I heard was a pilot in the air force and had supposedly died during the war. Danny had an Anglo surname but was considered a coyote, that is, a mixture of Anglo and Hispanic. The same thing was true at Santa Barbara School. Some students, such as Leo Sprunk and his brother Gene, with Anglo surnames, were also looked upon as coyotes. (Nowadays, Sprunk Road, west of the school, is named in honor of the Sprunk family.)

It was Sunday, a few days before celebrating Ash Wednesday, the first day of Lent—which lasted forty days. People honored certain traditions. In my family we didn't eat meat on Fridays or throughout Holy Week. And men like my father didn't shave until the Lenten Season had ended. It was hilarious to see all of them full-bearded in Mass. As for me, I vowed not to chew any gum throughout Lent.

That Sunday morning, I, and the rest of the family, returned from Mass at the San Ignacio Church. Since we had fasted, we were hungry and sat down to eat something. All of sudden there was some knocking on the screen door of our little house.

"Go see who it is, hijito," said Mom, and I half-opened the door. It was Pat, Danny, and a blond kid.

"Hey, dude!" uttered Pat. "Wanna go to the *mono* with us today?"

"And what is a mono?" I asked, while his buddies paced nervously back and forth.

"To the show," interrupted the blond kid, a bit impatient. "Holy shit! Where did this dumbo come from?" he remarked, with a hand over his mouth.

"By the way," exclaimed Danny, using a common expression among them, "this is Louie, Louie Nieves."

"Okay, Junie, what do you say? Going or not?" Pat added.

"First I have to ask my father permission to see if he'll let me go. Wait just a second. I'll be right back," I said, and closed the door.

"Who were they, hijito? What did they want?" asked Mom.

"They're Pat and Danny—you already know them—and a kid named Louie. They came to invite me to go with them to the show, but I told them that I have to ask Dad for permission."

A short discussion ensued between Mom and Dad. Then Dad went out and talked to the boys.

"Listen here. Junie can go with you, but I don't want him to get into any trouble. And how much is the show?"

"Twenty-five cents," responded Pat without hesitation. "Five cents for the show, ten cents for a soda and popcorn, and ten cents for the bus, coming and going."

Dad looked at Pat and then from the right-hand pocket of his Levi pants took out his leather coin purse. He carefully took out three five cent coins.

"Here you are: five cents for the show, five cents for the refreshment, and five cents for the popcorn."

"Dad. You forgot the money for the bus."

"Walk!" he said, without mincing his words. And the boys were left with their mouths open.

Evidently going to the movies was something that Pat and his buddies did often. As for me, I didn't have the slightest idea what a show was all about. Today that was ahead of me.

I said good-bye to Mom and Dad. She blessed me as usual, and I hugged her.

"Be careful, hijito. Don't go messing around."

We took off down the street where we lived till we got to Broadway. From here we walked to Mountain Road. We crossed the railroad tracks or the *traques*, as my partners would say. We even took shortcuts and one alley or another. Finally we got to La Mesa Theatre on Central Avenue, smack in the middle of downtown, about two or three miles from my little house. I was tired but excited when we got there.

After paying for the tickets, we bought refreshments and popcorn in the lobby. The second feature was about to begin. We stumbled in semi-darkness, trying to find empty seats. The theater was almost full of young people. Immediately it dawned upon me that the movies on Sunday afternoon were very popular among the boys and girls who lived in the barrios near downtown. They didn't stop talking, and very few were paying attention to the Looney Tunes.

Despite the semi-darkness, we finally found seats in the first row with a view looking straight up at the screen. I had never seen anything so colorful as Bugs Bunny and Porky Pig. And never in my life had I heard animals talk. Of course I talked to my rabbits and Bayito and Prieto, my two mounts at the ranch. They understood me although they didn't answer me.

As the film started a dead silence descended throughout the theater. The actors were Red Ryder and Little Beaver. All of a sudden I saw a bunch of horses galloping on the enormous screen. They came closer and closer. It looked as though they were going to trample me and turn me to dust, like the horses were raising. I became terribly frightened. I knew the damage wild horses could inflict on the poor human body. In a jiffy I stepped aside as if they were about to trample me and got under the seat in front of me. Pat and his buddies were laughing out loud. The other kids around us burst out laughing too. I didn't know what to think.

"Why were you hiding, Junie?" Pat whispered. "It's only a show. Nothing's going to happen. We come to the movies to have a good time."

I didn't say anything. We continued watching the movie. The only thing that could be heard apart from the characters and music from the film was my buddies. They munched on one kernel of popcorn at a time. From time to time they took a sip of their refreshment. All of that was new to me, and part of what I was learning outside the Santa Barbara confines.

I was fascinated with the photography because I had never seen cowboys and their mounts on the screen. I also understood little of their English. Their chatting in general was quite rapid.

While I concentrated on the movie I saw that Danny, Pat, and Louie barely paid attention to Red Ryder and Little Beaver. Little by little I realized that they, along with the majority of the boys and girls, had gone to the theater only to chitchat and have a good time. The murmuring around us was constant until the movie was over and the lights in the theater came on. At that instant there was shouting and more shouting.

"Hey dudes!" shouted Pat. "We must get the lead out. We're quite a ways from home."

"Did you like the show?" Danny asked me. "It was cool, huh?" This was an interesting comment, seeing that he, along with the majority of the young people, had not paid attention to the movie.

"Dudes," shouted Louie, who finally said something. "We still need to buy some *chuchulucos*."

"Chu, chuchu . . . what? What are you talking about?" I asked.

"Holy shit! Where did this guy come from? From hick country?" he commented in a whisper, although Pat heard him.

"Leave him alone, Louie. He hasn't been in Santa, the barrio, very long. He's new."

"Chuchulucos are candy," interrupted Danny. "Look. There they are," and I saw them but I didn't have money to buy any. They had money because they hadn't spent it on bus fare since we had walked to the movies.

With their money, they bought candy: Butterfingers, Almond

Joys, and Tootsie Rolls. They also bought gum: Bazooka Bubble Gum and Bubble Gum Cigars, all of them strange names to me.

"Okay, ready?" asked Pat. "We have a long ways to go to get home. I don't want my old man to get upset with me," he added, employing a term (in his lingo) here and there that I didn't understand.

"Or my old lady," said Danny, while I and Louie, the Wise Guy, uttered nary a word.

Before we started walking, Pat gave me a piece of his Butterfinger. Then we took off down Central Avenue until we reached First Street. Pat and Danny were in front and Louie and I followed. We ambled down one alley or another and crisscrossed the railroad tracks. We walked, chatted, and ate candy.

"Stop!" Louie yelled unexpectedly, and we stopped in the middle of the tracks. "Listen. Do you hear? The train," but you couldn't see anything. Nevertheless, we stepped to one side close to some red-brick buildings. Within a minute or two here came the train, whistling and spewing smoke. It flew by, raising dust and trash.

"Holy F . . . !" exclaimed Danny. "What if Louie hadn't heard the train."

"Don't be a drag. Here," Louie said, and he gave all of us a Bubble Gum Cigar.

Each one of us walked with a "cigar" in our mouth. Louie, Mr. Wise Guy, suddenly turned into a cutup. He pretended to puff on the Bubble Gum Cigar as if it were a real cigar. He pretended to blow smoke from his mouth and nose. Then he did something that totally surprised me. He started blowing bubbles: small ones, and others really huge. One of them burst and stuck to his nose and all over his face. I, along with Pat and Danny, burst out laughing. What a funny and entertaining sight!

We walked hopping, skipping, and jumping like the girls at the movies. We reached my little house, and I said good-bye to Pat, Louie, and Danny.

"Thanks for inviting me to the movies. It was out of sight! (*a toda eme*)!" They burst out laughing. I went indoors to see Mom and Dad. They were drinking coffee.

"Ah, hijito, you're back. How was the show? Did you have a good time?" Mom asked with a curious look on her face.

"Yes, Mom, I had a great time," I responded positively, with a twinkle in my eyes.

I shared my excitement with them, even though I was certain Mom hadn't quite understood everything since she herself had never seen a movie. I mentioned that we nibbled on popcorn and sipped soft drinks as we watched the cowboys and their mounts galloping on the screen. I told them as well about how much fun I had had coming home because with the money Pat and his pals had saved on bus fare, they'd bought plenty of candy to eat on the way home.

"Mom, I loved the chewy Tootsie Rolls, which I have never eaten. Here. I saved one for you." I gave Dad part of my Butterfinger.

"Would you like to go to the movies again?" Mom asked.

"Would I!" I responded with great enthusiasm.

"But you'll have to walk with your buddies," Dad uttered with a smile.

¿Quieres ir al mono?

POCA A POCO FUI conociendo a jóvenes como a Paloma y a muchachos de mi edad que vivían cerca o en la misma calle que yo. Dos de ellos eran Pat Perea y Danny Seiler cuyo padre oí decir era piloto en la fuerza aérea y es que murió durante la guerra. Danny tenía apellido anglo pero se le consideraba ser coyote, o sea, una mezcla de anglo e hispano. Lo mismo era verdad en la escuela de Santa Bárbara. Algunos estudiantes como Leo Sprunk y su hermano Gene con apellidos anglos también se les consideraba ser coyotes (Sprunk Road al oeste de la escuela hoy día lleva el nombre Sprunk en honor de la familia.).

Era domingo, unos días antes de celebrar el Miércoles de Ceniza, el primer día de la Cuaresma que duraba cuarenta días. La gente celebraba ciertas tradiciones. En mi familia no se comía carne los viernes o en la Semana Santa. Y los hombres como mi padre no se hacían la barba hasta acabarse la Cuaresma. Tenía gracia verlos en misa todos barbudos. Yo por mi parte dejaba de mascar chicle durante la Cuaresma.

Ese domingo por la mañana volvimos yo y el resto de la familia de misa en la Iglesia de San Ignacio. Siendo que habíamos ayunado, estábamos con hambre y nos sentamos todos a comer algo. De buenas a primeras se oyeron unos golpes en la puerta de alambre de nuestra casita.

—Mira a ver quién es, hijito—dijo mamá, y entre abrí la puerta. Eran Pat, Danny, y un güero.

—¡Órale!—dijo Pat—. ¿Quieres ir al mono hoy con nosotros?

—¿Y qué es mono?—pregunté mientras sus compañeros caminaban nerviosamente de un lado a otro.

—Al *show*—interrumpió el güero un poco impaciente—. ¡A la vechia! ¿De dónde vino este tapao?—comentó él tapándose la boca con una mano.

—*By the way*—exclamó Danny empleando expresión popular entre ellos—, éste es Louie, Louie Nieves. Bueno, Junie, ¿qué dices? ¿Vas o no vas?—añadió Pat.

—Primero tengo que pedirle permiso a mi apá pa ver si me deja ir. Espera un momentito. Ya vuelvo—y cerré la puerta.

—¿Quiénes eran hijito? ¿Qué querían?—preguntó mamá.

—Son Pat y Danny, ya tú los conocen, y un muchacho que se llama Louie. Vinieron a invitarme a que vaya con ellos al show, pero les dije que tengo que pedirle permiso a en papá.

Hubo una pequeña discusión entre papá y mamá. Luego salió él y les habló a los muchachos.

—Miren. El Junie puede ir con ustedes pero no quiero que se vaya a meter en bromas. ¿Y cuánto cuesta el show?

—Veinte y cinco centavos—contestó Pat sin pensarlo—. Cinco centavos para el show, diez centavos para una soda y *popcorn*, y diez centavos para la ida y vuelta en el bos.

Miró papá a Pat y entonces sacó de la bolsa derecha de sus pantalones Levi su portamonedas de piel. Con mucho cuidado sacó tres monedas de cinco centavos.

—Aquí tienes, cinco centavos para el show, cinco centavos para el refresco, y cinco centavos para las palomitas.

—Apá. Se te olvidó el dinero pal bos.

—¡Andar a pie!—prorrumpió sin medir sus palabras. Los muchachos se quedaron con la boca abierta.

Por lo visto que el ir al cine es algo que Pat y sus cuates hacían a menudo. Yo por mi parte no tenía ni la menor idea de qué se trataba un show. Hoy eso estaba por delante.

Me despedí de papá y mamá. Ella me echó la bendición, y yo le di un abrazo.

—Ten muncho cuidao, hijito. No vayas andar ahi traveseando.

Pescamos primero por la calle donde vivíamos hasta llegar a Broadway. De aquí fuimos andando hasta Mountain Road. Atravesamos las vías del ferrocarril o los traques como decían mis compañeros. Hasta tomamos atajos y uno que otro callejón. Por fin llegamos a La Mesa Theatre en la Calle Central en la mera Plaza a unas dos o tres millas de mi casita. Llegué cansado pero animado.

Después de pagar por los billetes, compramos refrescos y palomitas en el lobby. La segunda película (*second feature*) estaba por empezar. Tropezamos en la semioscuridad tratando de hallar sitios. El teatro estaba ya casi lleno de jóvenes. En seguida me di cuenta que el cine los domingos por la tarde era bastante popular entre los chicos y chicas que vivían en los barrios cerca del centro de la ciudad. No dejaban de hablar, y casi muy pocos le hacían caso a "Los Looney Tunes."

A pesar de la semioscuridad, al fin encontramos asientos en la primera fila con la vista hacia arriba bien cerca de la pantalla. Yo jamás había visto nada tan vistoso como "Bugs Bunny" y "Porky Pig." Y nunca en mi vida había oído a animales hablar. Claro que yo les hablaba a mis conejos y a Bayito y a Prieto mis monturas en el rancho. Ellos me entendían aunque no me contestaban.

Al empezar la película estalló un silencio muerto a través del teatro. Los actores eran "Red Ryder" y "Little Beaver." De buenas a primeras vi un montón de caballos galopeando en aquella pantalla enorme. Se acercaban cada vez más. Parecían que me iban a atropellar y dejarme hecho polvo como el que venían levantando las bestias. Me entró un miedo espantoso. Yo sabía el daño que podían hacerle caballos mesteños al pobre cuerpo humano. Así que en un decir amén me hice al lado como que estaban por atropellarme y me metí debajo del asiento en frente de mí. Pat y sus cuates estaban riéndose a carcajadas. Los otros chicos alrededor de nosotros también soltaron la risa. Yo no sabía qué pensar.

—¿Por qué te escondías, Junie?—preguntó Pat en voz baja—. No es más que el show. No pasa nada. Nosotros venimos al mono pa pasar un buen rato.

Yo no dije nada. Continuamos viendo la película. Lo único que se oía aparte de los personajes y la música de la película era mis compañeros. Ellos se ponían palomitas en la boca una por una. De vez en cuando tomaban un trago de su refresco. Todo aquello era una novedad para mí y parte de lo que venía aprendiendo en las afueras de Santa Bárbara.

Yo quedé fascinado con la fotografía porque jamás había visto vaqueros y sus monturas en la pantalla. Tampoco entendía poco del inglés. Su charla en general era bastante rápida.

Mientras me concentré en la película vi que Danny, Pat, y Louie apenas ponían atención a "Red Ryder" y "Little Beaver." Poco a poco me di cuenta que ellos junto con la mayoría de los chicos y chicas habían ido al cine solamente para charlar y pasar un buen rato. El murmureo alrededor de nosotros era constante hasta que se terminó la película y prendieron las luces del teatro. En ese instante hubo gritos y más gritos.

—¡Órale carnales!—gritó Pat—. Hay que darle cuerda al reló. Estamos bien lejos del chante.

—¿Te gustó el mono?—me preguntó Danny—. Estuvo ATM (A toda madre), ¿eh?—comentario interesante siendo que él junto con la mayoría de los jóvenes no le habían hecho caso a la película.

—Carnales— murmuró Louie que por fin dijo algo—. Nos falta comprar chuchulucos.

—¿Chu, chuchu . . . qué? ¿Qué dices?—le pregunté.

—¡A la vechia! ¿De dónde vino este camarada? ¿De la sierra?—comentó en voz baja aunque Pat lo oyó.

—Déjalo solo Louie. No hace muncho que vino a Santa, al barrio. Es nuevo.

—Chuchulucos son dulces—interrumpió Danny—. Mira. Ahi

están—y los vi pero yo no tenía dinero para comprar nada. Ellos sí porque no tuvieron que pagar para ir en el bos ya que vinimos a pie al cine.

Con su dinero compraron dulces: Butterfinger, Almond Joy, y Tootsie Rolls. También compraron chicle: Bazooka Bubble Gum y Bubble Gum Cigars, todos nombres raros para mí.

—Bueno, ¿listos?—declaró Pat—. Tenemos muncho que andar pa llegar al cantón. No quiero que se agüite mi jefe conmigo—añadió empleando una que otra palabra que yo no entendí.

—O mi jefita—añadió Danny, mientras que yo y Louie el Sábelotodo nos quedamos sin decir una palabra.

Antes de ponernos a caminar, me dio Pat parte de su Butterfinger. Luego pescamos por la Calle Central hasta llegar a la Calle Primera. Pat y Danny iban por delante y Louie y yo detrás.

Pescamos por uno que otro callejón y entrecruzamos los traques. Fuimos andando, charlando y comiendo dulces.

—¡Párense!—chilló inesperadamente Louie, y nos paramos en medio de los traques—. Escuchen. ¿Oyen? El tren—pero no se veía nada. Sin embargo, nos hicimos a un lado cerca de unos edificios de ladrillos colorados. Dentro de uno o dos minutos aquí viene el tren, pitando y echando humo. Pasó volando, levantando polvo y basura.

¡A la chingada!—exclamó Danny—. Que si no hubiera oído Louie el tren.

—No se agüiten. Tengan—dijo Louie y nos dio a todos nosotros un Bubble Gum Cigar.

Seguimos cada uno con un "puro" en la boca. Louie el Majadero de buenas a primeras se convirtió en un payaso. Pretendía chuparse el Gum Cigar como si de veras fuera un puro. Pretendía echar humo por la boca y la nariz. Luego hizo algo que me sorprendió por completo. Se puso a hacer globos, unos chiquitos y otros bien grandes. Uno de ellos se explotó y se le pegó en la nariz y por toda la cara. Yo junto con Pat y Danny soltamos la risa. ¡Qué espectáculo más gracioso y divertido!

Caminos dando saltos juguetones como las chicas que vi en el cine. Llegamos a mi casita, y me despedí de Pat, Louie, y Danny.

—Gracias por invitarme al mono. ¡Estuvo A Toda Eme!—. Soltaron ellos la risa. Entré a ver a mamá y a papá. Estaban bebiendo café.

—Ah, hijito, ya volvites. ¿Cómo estuvo el show? ¿Tuvites buen tiempo?—preguntó mamá con una cara de curiosidad.

—Sí, amá. Tuve un buen tiempo—contesté seguro que con un brillo en los ojos.

Compartí mi entusiasmo con ellos, aunque estaba seguro que mamá no había comprendido del todo siendo que ella misma nunca había visto una película. Mencioné que comimos palomitas de maíz and bebimos refrescos mientras mirábamos a los vaqueros y sus monturas galopando en la pantalla. Les dije también del buen rato que tuve camino a casa porque con el dinero que Pat y sus compañeros ahorraron del viaje en autobús compraron bastantes dulces para comer camino a casa.

—Amá, me encantaron los gomosos Tootsie Rolls que yo jamás había probado. Toma. Guardé uno para ti—. A papá le di parte de mi Butterfinger.

—¿Te gustaría ir al show otra vez?—preguntó mamá.

—¡Qué si me gustaría!—respondí con gran entusiasmo.

—Pero tendrás que andar a pie con tus cuates—dijo papá con una sonrisa.

Borrego

BORREGO WASN'T A BUDDY of mine. I met him one day after school. Borrego, that's what they called him. And little wonder. He had wooly hair like a lamb. But his hair wasn't the only thing that attracted attention. It was the way he talked. When Borrego spoke Spanish, his elders listened but they understood little of what he said. They were left speechless.

The opposite occurred among the majority of young people in the barrio where I lived. They comprehended Borrego's prattle. As for me, a newcomer, I tried to understand him but it was not easy. At the very least I pretended to grasp what he was saying. I didn't want him and his buddies to think that I was a country bumpkin from Tajique.

Friday afternoon was upon us and Mrs. Padilla, our teacher at Santa Barbara, dismissed her class early. Lauro "Loro" Crespín, a friend of mine who came from San Ysidro, close to Jémez Springs, invited me to share a soda pop with him at his parents' store, Tom's Grocery, named after his father. The store was next to the school.

"Dad, Mom, I want you to meet Junie. He and I are in the same class. I invited him to have a soft drink," Loro said, and he fetched a pop from a small footlocker full of blocks of ice.

"Take a sip."

"Boy is it good! What is it?"

"It's Nehi," Loro answered. "Strawberry-flavored. It's the best soda pop there is. I like it very much."

The words had barely escaped his mouth when three boys walked in. I quickly saw that they were dressed rather oddly—not like the students at Santa Barbara School. Their pants were tight at the ankles and baggy up to the waistline. They looked like they were puffed full of air. One of the boys also had his collar turned up.

"Hey Loro!" Borrego hollered. "I want some smokes and matches for my old man. He gets grumpy if he doesn't have something to puff on. Who's this dude with cat eyes who doesn't stop gawking at me?"

"His name is Junie. He's a buddy of mine. He just moved to the barrio. And what really brings you to Santa?" Loro asked Borrego without mincing words.

"I came to see Betty. I heard a dude from this neck of the woods wants to monkey around with her. Listen here, bro. You have to be on your toes. If not they'll take your chick away."

"And are you still at San Jo School?" Loro queried.

"No dude. They expelled me because the principal caught me smoking a joint in the shithouse. Okay. See you later," Borrego said, and he and his pals took off.

"Wow, Loro! Is that the way Borrego talks all the time? I barely understood what he said."

"Look, Junie. I too don't understand all that wordiness. That's the way the *chucos*, zoot-suiters talk, but I pretend to know what they say."

"And what are zuit-sooters?"

"*Pachucos*. Sooner or later you'll learn."

"And did you see Borrego's pants all puffed up?"

"Yes. And do you know what my father calls them? Fart retainers."

"Ah, ja, ja! Your father's funny."

"But why does Borrego have white hair?"

"Ah, good question, Junie. It's because he dyes it. He wants his hair to be real white like lamb's wool."

"And who gave him that nickname?"

"No one knows for sure, but a man in the barrio is famous for giving nicknames to young people like Borrego."

"Okay, that's enough questions. I have to head home. I don't want Mom to be worried. See you later."

"Look, Junie. If you're going to learn the chuco lingo you don't say 'home.' It's *chante* or *cantón*. Oh, by the way, the San Ignacio fiestas in Martíneztown are this weekend. I'm going Saturday afternoon with my *jefitos*, old folks. You wanna come with us?"

"Why not, but I have to ask my parents' permission. If they say yes, I'll go."

"I'll stop by your house on Saturday after lunch. What do you say?"

"Fine, Loro. Let's see what my parents say," and I went home.

I found Mom at the small table where we eat. She was feeding my little sister Elsie, who was barely a year old.

"What a surprise! I didn't expect you till later."

"Yes, Mom. Mrs. Padilla let us out early. Then I went with my friend Loro to drink a soda pop. And you're not going to believe this. There I met this boy, Borrego."

"What kind of a name is that?" Mom asked.

"Ah, it's because he has wooly hair like a lamb. But not only that, he also dyes his hair white."

"And how old is this Borrego?"

"I don't know, but he's older than me and skinny as a stick. Oh yes. Before I forget. Saturday, Loro is coming over to invite me to go with him and his parents to the San Ignacio fiestas."

"Fine with me, but you'll have to ask your father if you can go."

At supper Mom reminded Dad that the San Ignacio fiestas were that weekend.

"Yes. How can I forget? They're always in July."

"And would you like to go, dear?" Mom asked.

"Why not? That way I can try out my new boots."

"And I can wear my new dress that you bought me," Mom smiled.

"We can both go looking dapper," Dad added.

These last words really surprised Mom seeing that Dad was very careful, even in what he said to her.

Before I knew it, Saturday was here. We had hardly finished lunch when I heard a knock on the screen door.

"Go see who it is, hijito," said Mom.

"It's Loro, my friend from school."

"Well, tell him to come in."

"Good afternoon, Mrs. López. I came to see if Junie can go with me and my parents to the fiestas."

"Yes, he already told us you're going," said Mom. "We're going too, but later. Junie's going with us. We'll see you there."

"See you later, alligator," Loro said, and waved good-bye to me.

In the evening my parents and I went to the five o'clock Mass. Going to Mass in Martíneztown was very important to Mom. She never forgets that it was in the San Ignacio Church where she and Dad were married. Upon leaving the church, the first thing you heard was music.

"Do you hear, dear?" Mom said to Dad. "The band is playing. I feel like dancing."

"Fine with me, but you know how my feet get all tangled up when I dance," Dad warned her.

"It doesn't matter, dear. Drag your feet however you can, but at least you'll break in your boots, don't you think?" And Mom cracked a smile.

The dance was in a large tent not far from the church. There were chairs all around inside for people to sit. Other guests stood outside listening to the band, or they danced. We sat close to the musicians. A little later Loro and his parents arrived. He came over to see me.

"Hey dude!"

"What's up, Loro? You remember my parents, right?"

"Of course! Can Junie come with me to make the rounds? We'll be back in a little while."

"Okay, but don't go get into any trouble," Dad cautioned us, and we took off. First we stopped at a food stand.

"You want a cotton candy?" Loro asked.

"What's that?"

"You'll see. Here. Taste it. You like it?"

"Boy it's good! But it melts very quickly in your mouth."

"Because it's pure sugar."

Suddenly Loro covered his right ear with his hand, which caught my attention.

"Listen. Do you hear? It's the Chavos band. I know their music. Do you remember Borrego?"

"How can I forget."

"Well, Borrego and the Chavos are buddies. Let's go listen to them. They have their own tent near here."

As we arrived, Borrego and some guys and gals were huddled together.

"Hey Loro!" hollered Borrego. "I want you to meet Betty, my chick. She's got a beauty shop near Saint Joseph's Hospital next to Longfellow School. That's where I go with all the old farts so Betty—and he hugs her with one arm—can fix me up, like out of sight. Okay, see you later, alligator. Betty and I are going to go dance up a storm."

I could only scratch my head, listening to all of Borrego's crowing. Loro and I then got close to the tent to listen to los Chavos and to watch Borrego and Betty dance. They and other couples danced, turned around with their arms above their head, and then made more twists with a strong stomping of the heels. I was surprised.

"What do you think, Junie? Do you like what you see?" Loro asked.

"Yes and no. I've never seen that kind of dancing."

"It's the jitterbug, a popular dance among the chucos. Los Chavos are known for playing the jitter."

No sooner had they finished playing the number when a group of six or seven chucos in typical garb—loose shirts, puffed up pants, and black shiny shoes—showed up. One of them was dressed totally in black.

"Holy shit!" Loro shrieked. "There's going to be trouble. See the chuco in the black suit, black shoes, and black hat? He's from San Jo and is very popular among the girls. His name is el Perico because he has a long and pointed nose. He's always looking for trouble and picks on guys who have a girlfriend, like Borrego."

"Hey Borrego! Of all the sheep, I'm the one and only shepherd (i.e., lover) to whom all the chicks flock," exclaimed Perico. "That's why I've come to take Betty out to dance so she and I can dance up a storm."

"Fuck off," says Borrego. "Betty's with me."

"Watch out, watch out for Perico," shouted someone in Borrego's group. "He's got a knife. He's got a knife."

"There's gonna be a rumble and you're gonna tumble," Perico said to Borrego. "You see this knife?" And he waved it in the air. "With it I'm going to cut your balls so that you can't stick your stick in your Betty."

No sooner had he spewed his insulting words than all hell broke loose between the two gangs. Fisticuffs came and went and kicks flew in the air, with knives sparkling in mid-fight. Screams were heard.

"The police, the police!" Everyone ran in all directions. Borrego held onto Betty's hand. He barely escaped from having a knife stuck in his belly.

"Let's go, let's go!" I shouted to Loro. "Or else my parents are going to be worried."

"Calm down, calm down, Junie!"

I found Mom and Dad seated under the adults' tent listening to polkas, waltzes, and rancheras. They had stopped dancing, since Dad's feet hurt due to his new boots. All of a sudden, much to Mom's surprise, the band started playing "La Chaparrita," one of her favorite Mexican songs. She sang it at the ranch whenever

Dad left for five days on Monday mornings to go work for the WPA.

"Dear, let's do this last number. You know how much I love 'La Chaparrita.' Then we can go home."

They waltzed to the beautiful song whose words I also knew by heart.

Adiós mi chaparrita,
no llores por tu Pancho.
Que si se va del rancho,
muy pronto volverá,
muy pronto volverá.
///
Farewell my dear Chaparrita,
don't cry for your Pancho.
Why, if he leaves the ranch,
he shall return quite soon,
he shall return quite soon.

The band finished playing and Mom tapped me on the shoulder.

"Let's go home, hijito. Your dad's tired."

We left for home shortly thereafter. Mom also was tired but very happy since she had been able to dance and wear her new dress for the first time.

Monday morning I left early for school. I didn't want to be late. I went into the classroom. Mrs. Padilla hadn't arrived but a few schoolmates were huddled in one corner. I saw Loro.

"What's up, Junie? I bet you don't know what happened at the fiestas."

"Besides the fights?"

"The police jailed Borrego but Betty has already got him out. She paid the bail or whatever."

Sooner or later more was learned about what had transpired.

For sure, Borrego had to promise Betty two things. She demanded that he give up the gangs in the barrio, and, to dedicate himself to haircutting, like her. If not, he would have to find another girlfriend. Borrego promised to fulfill her wishes.

Like the strong ditch current that ran through Santa Barbara and Martíneztown, gossip spread fast all over the whole barrio. Soon it became known that Borrego was no longer commingling with his pals from San Jo. Rather, he was attending barber school in Santa Fe. Within six weeks Borrego returned as an intern at Betty's Hair Salon. Upon finishing his apprenticeship, Betty and Borrego got married and renamed her salon. They named it B and B's Salon, where nowadays many of Betty's clients go, as well as Borrego's friends.

Borrego likes to brag jokingly that now he doesn't have to pay to have his hair dyed. Coloring his hair white is one thing that hasn't changed in him, and Betty does not object. They both lead a happy life in Martíneztown with their two *borreguitos* (lambs), as Borrego calls them.

Borrego

BORREGO NO ERA CUATE mío. Yo lo conocí un día después de clases. Borrego, así le llamaban. Y con razón. Tenía el pelo lanudo como un borrego. Pero su pelo no era lo único que llamaba la atención. Era su manera de hablar. Cuando Borrego hablaba español los mayores escuchaban pero entendían poco de lo que decía. Se quedaban con la boca abierta.

Todo lo contrario ocurría con la mayoría de los jóvenes en el barrio donde yo vivía. Ellos comprendían el palabreo de Borrego. En cuanto a mí un recién llegado, yo trataba de entenderlo pero me costaba trabajo. Por lo menos me hacía como que captaba lo que él decía. No quería que él y sus compañeros creyeran que yo era un serreño de Tajique.

El viernes por la tarde estaba ante nosotros y nuestra maestra la Sra. Padilla en Santa Bárbara despachó su clase temprano. Lauro (Loro) Crespín, amigo mío de San Ysidro cerca de Jémez, me convidó a compartir una soda con él en la tienda de sus padres, *Tom's Grocery* nombrada en honor de su papá. La tienda estaba a un lado de la escuela.

—Papá, mamá quiero que conozcan a Junie. Él y yo estamos en la mesma clase. Lo convidé a tomar un refresco—y sacó Loro una soda de una petaquilla llena de bloques de hielo.

—Tómate un trago.

—¡Y qué suave está! ¿Qué es?

—Es *Nehi*—contestó Loro—. De sabor a fresa. Es la mejor soda que hay. A mí me gusta muncho.

Apenas se le escapó la última palabra cuando entraron tres muchachos. Pronto vi que andaban vestidos de una manera extraña y no como los estudiantes en la Escuela de Santa Bárbara. Sus pantalones estaban apretados en los tobillos y guangudos hasta la cintura. Parecía que estaban llenos de aire. Uno de los chicos también llevaba el cuello parado.

—¡Órale Loro!—gritó Borrego—. Queiro unos frajos y trolas pa mi jefito. Se agüita si no tiene que chupar. ¿Quién es este vato con ojos de gato que no deja de mirarme?

—Se llama Junie. Es mi camarada. Acaba de mudarse al barrio. ¿Y qué de veras te trae por Santa?—le preguntó Loro a Borrego sin pelos en la lengua.

—Vine a ver a la Betty. Oí que un vato de por acá quiere monquiar con ella. Mira carnal. Tienes que ponerte truchas ése. Si no te quitan tu chava.

—¿Y que toavía vas a la escuela en San Jo?—. Le preguntó Loro.

—Nel ése. Me hicieron *expel* porque el principal me pescó sonándome un leño en el cagadero—dijo Borrego—. Güeno. Ai te guacho—y se despidieron él y sus camaradas.

—¡Híjole Loro! ¿Qué asina habla siempre Borrego? Apenas entendí lo que dijo.

—Mira Junie. Yo tampoco entiendo todo ese enredo de palabras. Asina hablan los chucos, pero yo me hago como que sé lo que dicen.

—¿Y qué son chucos?

—Pachucos. Con el tiempo sabrás.

—¿Y vites los calzones de Borrego todos esponjados?

—Sí. ¿Y sabes cómo los llama mi jefito? Guarda pedos.

—¡Ah ja, ja! Qué chistoso es tu papá.

—¿Pero por qué Borrego tiene el pelo blanco?

—Ah, buena pregunta Junie. Es porque se lo tiñe. Quiere que el pelo esté bien blanco como la lana diun borrego.

—¿Y quién le puso ese sobrenombre?

—No se sabe por cierto, pero un hombre en el barrio tiene fama de ponerles sobrenombres a jóvenes como Borrego.

—Güeno, ya basta de preguntas. Tengo que irme a casa. No quiero que vaya a estar mi amá con la pena. Ai te guacho.

—Mira Junie. Si vas a aprender chuco no se dice casa. Es chante o cantón. Oh, *by the way*, este fin de semana se celebran las fiestas de San Ignacio en Martíneztown. Yo voy el sábado por la tarde con mis jefitos. ¿Quieres venir con nosotros?

—Como que no, pero tengo que pedirles permiso a mis padres. Si me dejan ir, voy.

—Yo paso por tu casa el sábado después del lonche. ¿Qué dices?

—Güeno Loro. A ver qué dicen mis padres—y me fui a casa.

Hallé a mamá en la mesita donde comemos. Estaba dándole de comer a mi hermanita Elsie que apenas tenía un año.

—¡Qué sorpresa! No te esperaba hasta más tarde.

—Sí amá. La Sra. Padilla nos dejó ir a casa temprano. Luego jui con mi amigo Loro a beber una soda. Y no vas a creer lo que te digo. Ahi conocí a este muchacho Borrego.

—¿Qué clase de nombre es ése?—preguntó mamá.

—Ah, es porque tiene el pelo lanudo como un borrego. Pero no sólo eso, tamién se tiñe el cabello blanco.

—¿Y cuántos años tiene este Borrego?

—No sé pero es mayor que yo y delgado como un palo. Ah sí. Antes que se me olvide. El sábado viene Loro a convidarme pa que vaya con él y sus padres a las fiestas de San Ignacio.

—Está bien conmigo, pero tendrás que preguntarle a tu papá si puedes ir.

Para la cena le recordó mamá a papá que las fiestas de San Ignacio eran ese fin de semana.

—Sí. Cómo se me han de olvidar. Siempre son en julio.

—¿Y te gustaría ir, viejo?—. Le preguntó mamá.

—Por qué no. Asina puedo estrenar mis botas nuevas.

—Y yo puedo estrenar mi túnico nuevo que me comprates—. Se sonrió mamá.

—Podemos ir los dos bien panteras—añadió papá.

Estas últimas palabras sí que sorprendieron a mamá siendo que papá era muy cuidadoso hasta en lo que le decía a ella.

Cuando menos pensé, el sábado estaba por encima. Apenas acabábamos de lonchar cuando oí unos golpes en la puerta de alambre.

—Ve a ver quién es hijito—dijo mamá.

—Es Loro, mi amigo de la escuela.

—Pues dile que pase.

—Buenas tardes Sra. López. Vine a ver si puede ir el Junie conmigo y mis padres a las fiestas.

—Sí, ya nos dijo que ustedes van—dijo mamá—. Nosotros tamién vamos pero más tarde. El Junie va con nosotros. Allá te veremos.

—Ai te guacho más tarde—dijo Loro y se despidió de mí.

Por la tarde fuimos yo y mis padres a la misa de las cinco. Ir a misa para mamá en Martíneztown era muy importante. Nunca se le olvida que fue en la Iglesia de San Ignacio donde se casaron ella y papá. Al salir de la iglesia lo primero que se oía era música.

—¿Oyes viejo?—le dice mamá a papá—. Está tocando la banda. Tengo ganas de bailar.

—Está bien conmigo, pero ya tú sabes cómo se me traban las patas cuando bailo—le advirtió papá.

—No importa querido. Arrastra las patas como puedas, pero por lo menos quebrantas las botas, ¿qué no?—y se sonrió mamá.

El baile era en una carpa grande no muy lejos de la iglesia. Había sillas todo alrededor por dentro para que se sentara la gente. Otros huéspedes estaban fuera de pie escuchando la banda o salían a bailar. Nosotros nos sentamos cerca de los músicos. Poco después llegaron Loro y sus padres. Vino él a verme.

—¡Órale vato!

—¿Qué tal Loro? Te acuerdas de mis padres, ¿no?

—¡Cómo no! ¿Puede ir el Junie a dar la vuelta conmigo? Volvemos en un ratito.

—Güeno, pero no se vayan a meter en bromas—nos advirtió papá y nos fuimos andando. Primero paramos en un vendible.

—¿Quieres algodón de azúcar?—me preguntó Loro.

—¿Qué es eso?

—Ya verás. Toma. Pruébalo. ¿Te gusta?

—¡Qué suave está! Pero se derrite muy pronto en la boca.

—Porque es pura azúcar.

De pronto Loro se tapó con una mano la oreja derecha, lo cual me llamó la atención.

—Escucha. ¿Oyes? Es la banda de los Chavos. Yo conozco su música. ¿Te acuerdas de Borrego?

—Cómo se me puede olvidar.

—Pues Borrego y los Chavos son compas. Vamos a escucharlos. Ellos tienen su propia carpa cerca de aquí.

Al llegar, Borrego y otra plebe estaban hechos bola.

—¡Órale Loro!—gritó Borrego—. Quiero que conozcas a la Betty, mi chava. Ella tiene un *beauty shop* cerca del Hospital de San José a un lado de la Escuela Longfellow. Allá voy yo con todos los rucos y rucas pa que Betty—y la abraza con un brazo— me ponga de aquellas. Güeno, ai te guacho. Betty y yo vamos a tirar chancla.

Yo solamente me rascaba la cabeza con todo aquel cacareo de Borrego. Entonces Loro y yo nos acercamos a la carpa para escuchar a los Chavos y a ver bailar a Borrego y a la Betty. Ellos y otras parejas bailaban. Se daban vueltas con los brazos por encima de la cabeza, y luego más vueltas con fuertes taconazos. Yo me quedé sorprendido.

—¿Qué tal Junie? ¿Te gusta lo que ves?—me pregunta Loro.

—Sí y no. Jamás he visto esa clase de baile.

—Es el *jitterbug*, baile popular de los chucos. Los Chavos tienen fama de tocar el *jitter*.

Nomás en cuanto acabaron la pieza y un grupo de seis o siete chucos con sus trajes típicos, o sea, camisa guanga, pantalones soplados, y zapatos negros relumbrosos se plantaron. Uno de ellos andaba vestido completamente de negro.

—¡A la vequia!—gritó Loro—. Va haber pedo. ¿Ves el chuco con tacuche negro, calcos negros, y sombrero negro? Él es de San Jo y tiene fama entre las chavalas. Se llama el Perico porque tiene una nariz larga y puntiaguda. Siempre busca pleito con otros chavos que tienen novia como Borrego.

—¡Órale Borrego! De todas las borregas soy yo el mero borreguero a quien todas las chavalas se acercan—exclamó el Perico—. Por eso vengo a sacar a la Betty pa dar ella y yo un vuelazo.

—Ni a tu madre—le dice Borrego—. La Betty anda conmigo.

—¡Truchas, truchas con el Perico!—gritó uno del grupo de Borrego—. Trae filero. Trae filero.

—Va haber retumbos por todos rumbos—le dijo el Perico a Borrego—. ¿Ves esta fila?—y la movió en el aire—.Con ella te voy a cortar las bolas pa que no le metas palo a tu Betty.

No acabaron de escupírsele sus palabras de insultos cuando se armó la gorda entre las dos pandillas. Volaban jodazos y patadas con una que otra navaja que relumbraba en el aire. Se oyeron gritos.

—¡La jura, la jura!—. Salieron todos corriendo por todos rumbos. Borrego agarró a la Betty de la mano. A penas se escapó él de que le metieran una navaja en la panza.

—¡Vamos, vamos!—le grité a Loro—. O mis padres van a estar con la pena.

—¡Cálmate, cálmate Junie!

Hallé a papá y a mamá sentaditos en la carpa de los mayores escuchando polcas, valses, y rancheras. Habían dejado de bailar ya que le dolían los pies a papá a causa de sus botas nuevas. De pronto, lo cual sorprendió a mamá, la banda empezó a tocar "La Chaparrita," una de sus canciones favoritas mexicanas. Ella la cantaba en el rancho al despedirse papá por cinco días los lunes por la mañana para ir a trabajar en el WPA.

—Viejo, vamos a bailar esta última pieza. Ya sabes lo mucho que me gusta "La Chaparrita." Luego nos vamos a casa.

Bailaron la bonita canción cuyas palabras yo también me sabía de memoria.

Adiós mi chaparrita,
no llores por tu Pancho.
Que si se va del rancho,
muy pronto volverá,
muy pronto volverá.

La banda acabó de tocar y mamá me tocó el hombro.

—Vámonos a casa, hijito. Tú papá está cansado.

Poco después nos fuimos. Mamá también estaba cansada pero muy contenta ya que pudo bailar y estrenar su túnico nuevo.

El lunes por la mañana me fui temprano a la escuela para no llegar tarde. Entré en el aula. La Sra. Padilla todavía no llegaba pero unos escueleros estaban hechos bolas en un rincón. Vi a Loro.

—¿Qué hay Junie? ¿A que no sabes lo que pasó en las fiestas?

—¿Aparte de las peleas?

—La jura entabicó a Borrego pero ya la Betty lo sacó. Ella pagó la fianza o no sé qué.

Tarde o temprano se supo más de lo que pasó. Por cierto, Borrego tuvo que prometerle a la Betty dos cosas. Ella le demandó que dejara las gavillas en el barrio, y, que se dedicara a cortar pelo como ella. Si no, que se buscara él a otra novia. Borrego prometió cumplir con sus deseos.

Como la fuerte corriente de la acequia que corría por Santa Bárbara y Martíneztown, el mitote corrió rápido por todo el barrio. Pronto se supo que Borrego ya no andaba con sus compañeros de San Jo sino que estaba en Santa Fe asistiendo a una escuela para peluqueros. Dentro de seis semanas Borrego regresó como interno a la peluquería de Betty. Al terminar su aprendizaje, Betty y Borrego se casaron y renombraron su salón. Le pusieron el nombre Salón B y B a donde hoy día van muchos clientes de Betty como también amigos de Borrego.

A Borrego le gusta jactarse de una manera chistosa que ahora no tiene que pagar para que le tiñan el pelo. Tiñéndose el pelo blanco es lo único que no ha cambiado en él, y la Betty no se opone. Los dos llevan una vida alegre en Martíneztown con sus dos "borreguitos" (así los llama Borrego).

Quico and Quica

BORREGO AND BETTY LED a happy life, but their lifestyle, compared to Quico and Quica's, was quite different. Quica was married to Quico, ten years younger than she. Though younger, he had his jealous moments, and little wonder. Besides being tall, his wife was a very attractive redhead with blue eyes. As for him, he was neither handsome nor bad-looking but short and chubby. Whenever they went for a stroll, shopping or whatever, everybody noticed their height differences—something that didn't please Quico, to say the least. Despite everything, they had been married for years and were very much in love.

Only a few days remained before his wife's birthday. He started thinking. What gift could he give her? He was tired of chocolates, bouquets of flowers, and other niceties. This time he wanted to surprise her with something new and different. He could think of nothing.

One day, Quico headed for La Plaza, downtown Albuquerque, to see Diego, the pharmacist at B. (Bernard) Ruppe Drugstore, about renewing a prescription. On the way home he stopped for a few moments to say hello to his good friend David Orozco at Oro's Barbershop on Mountain Road, not far from the two-story house where the politician Licho Martínez lived.*

* To learn more about the Martínez clan, please consult *La voz de mi conciencia: Life, Times, and Talents of Luis S. Martínez* by Demetria Martínez with Enrique Lamadrid and Teodoro Martínez.

After bidding good-bye to David, Quico paused at the AAA Bird Shop on Broadway Boulevard, next to the Archuletas' AAA Merchant Store. In the storefront he saw a few birds on their perches. Some were chirping or pecking at seeds and eating them. The birds all had different-colored and shiny plumage. Quico thought for a moment. He scratched his head. The more he contemplated that scene, the more it became embedded in his head that perhaps a nice gift, something unexpected and surprising, would be a bird. "Why not?" he said to himself, and he went into the AAA Bird Shop.

"Good morning," was the cordial greeting from a tall man with a moustache. "What can I do for you, sir?"

"Well, I don't know exactly. Perhaps you can help me."

"Gladly. I'm Bonifacio, the owner. Everybody calls me Boni. Now then, what did you have in mind?"

Quico proceeded to explain to him the years he had been married to his wife and the fact that he was tired of giving her chocolates and flowers for her birthday. The time to surprise her with something different and original was upon him.

"Incidentally, what is your name?" Bonifacio asked.

"Quico. My wife and I live in the Santa Barbara neighborhood not far from here."

"Bingo!" he shouted out of the blue. "I know just what you can give your dear wife for her birthday."

"You don't say!"

"A parrot," proposed the owner with a wry smile. "What do you think? What's more, *perico* rhymes with Quico, ha, ha," he added, which Quico thought was funny. "Not only that; I have a parrot that talks. Okay, he at least says two or three words. Come. I'll show him to you. There he is. What do you think?"

The parrot was beautiful. It had glittering green plumage. According to the owner, he was barely a year and a half old. He also assured Quico that in due time the parrot would be able to learn additional words.

"And what words does he know?" Quico asked.

"I love you," replied Bonifacio without hesitation.

"Perfect! The words 'I love you' say it all. And how much do you want for him? But don't go charge me an arm and a leg," Quico cautioned him kiddingly.

"No, no, no. I'll let you have him cheap. Two dollars."

"It's a deal," exclaimed Quico, and he took out a wrinkled one-dollar bill from his coin purse along with four two-bit coins. "Here you are," he said, and Bonifacio fetched the parrot from the cage to hand to Quico.

"And does the parrot bite or not?"

"Well, all parrots peck. It's part of their nature. They peck to eat, they peck to . . ."

"Then you'll have to donate me the cage," interrupted Quico. "If not, give me back my money because I can't turn the parrot loose in my workshop." (Quico was known for his workmanship in leather.)

"Look, seeing that you live nearby and are a neighbor, you don't have to give me a penny for the cage. I'm even going to give you a small sack of seeds for you to feed him. They'll last a few days."

"Thank you very much. You're very kind."

Quico left the store happy as a lark. He moved the cage and parrot from one hand to the other as he walked, in order not to get tired. He whistled like a kid as he ambled down the street until he reached home. Now came the good part. How to enter his workshop behind the house without having Quica seeing or hearing him? "It's a good thing we don't have a dog," he thought to himself. He entered on his tiptoes and hung the cage from a beam in his workshop.

He left his workshop quietly and went into the house through the porch that faced Edith Boulevard and the Santa Barbara Cemetery.

"My dear," said Quica upon seeing him. "Why did you take so long? I was worried about you," and she hugged him.

"Well, coming and going on foot to town as old as I am takes time. On the way back I stopped to see my friend David Orozco where I always got my hair cut."

"Would you like a cup of coffee?"

"Yes, of course!"

"Here you are dear, coffee with milk the way you like it . . . and two *bizcochitos* for you to dunk. I just made them," and she kissed her husband on the forehead.

There were still three days before Quica's birthday. In the meantime, Quico spent the mornings in his workshop. He was used to his wife not bothering him. In that way he was able to feed the parrot and give it water without her noticing. The only thing is that every time Quico entered his workshop the parrot repeated, "I love you. I love you," which made him laugh.

Finally it was Friday, Quica's birthday. Quico, besides being handy in leatherwork, also cooked a very tasty chicken and rice. That's what he prepared for his dear wife to honor her birthday. For dessert there were delicious *natillas* that a next-door neighbor brought her.

"My love, your chicken and rice, as always, were finger-licking good. Thanks, my dear."

"On the contrary. Thanks to you for being such a good wife throughout the years . . . wait for just a brief moment. I have a surprise for you," he said, and he returned with the cage covered with an old blue shirt of his. "Happy Birthday!" declared Quico aloud. "Here you are." No sooner had he uncovered the cage than the parrot spewed those adorable words: "I love you, I love you." Quica laughed. She thought the parrot was funny.

"Oh, my goodness! A parrot that talks. What a surprise!" and she embraced her husband.

"Do you like him?"

"Yes, and what I like the most at first sight are the truly green feathers. They remind me of the green dress that you gave me for our tenth anniversary some years back. I still have it."

"Okay, now you have to decide where to put your friend," Quico smiled.

"Well, during the day we can put him in the portal and at night we'll bring him inside the house. What do you think?"

"Good," said Quico. "Now comes the good part. What name do you wish to give the parrot? He must have a name. We can't keep calling him parrot."

"That's a lot more difficult. I'll have to think of a good name."

A few days went by. Nothing came to Quica's mind. She pondered, but nothing came into her head. One morning she got up at the crack of dawn. Wham! "Why not name him Sol?" she said to herself.

Quico had just gotten up and he went into the kitchen half asleep, rubbing his eyes.

"Good morning, dear. Better late than never, ha," and she gave him a cup of coffee with milk. "Well, today it's me that has a surprise."

"Don't tell me. What surprise can it be at these early hours of the morning?"

"I have a name for the parrot. Sol!"

"Ah, I like it. And what made you think of that name?"

"It was easy," she said with a smile. "At the crack of dawn this morning I thought of you, my love. You are the sun that brightens my life day after day. And not only that, I now have two loves—you and Sol. You two say to me, 'I love you, I love you.' What else is left?"

Quico excused himself and returned at once with Sol and the bird cage and handed both to Quica.

"I love you, I love you," repeated Sol.

"I love her as well," added Quico, as a tear trickled down each one of Quica's cheeks.

Quico y Quica

BORREGO Y BETTY LLEVARON una vida alegre, pero su estilo de vida comparado al de Quico y Quica fue bastante diferente. Quica estaba casada con Quico, hombre diez años menor que ella. Aunque era más joven, él tenía sus celos, y con razón. Además de ser alta, ella era una pelirroja muy guapa con ojos azules. En cuanto a él, no era guapo ni feo pero chaparro y gordito. Cuando salían de paseo, de compras o cosas por el estilo, todo el mundo se fijaba en la estatura de cada uno, algo que no le agradaba a Quico, ni mucho menos. A pesar de todo, llevaban años casados y estaban muy enamorados.

Faltaban apenas unos días para el cumpleaños de su esposa. Se puso a pensar. ¿Qué regalo le podría regalar? Estaba cansado de brindarle chocolates, ramilletes de flores, u otros agrados. Esta vez quería sorprenderla con algo nuevo y diferente. Nada le venía a la mente.

Un día se fue andando Quico para La Plaza, el centro de Albuquerque, a ver a Diego, el boticario en la Botica B. (Bernard) Ruppe, para renovar una receta. Camino a casa se detuvo por unos momentos en la Peluquería Oro para saludar a su buen amigo David Orozco en Mountain Road. no muy lejos de la casa de dos pisos donde vivía el político Licho Martínez.

Tras despedirse de David, Quico paró unos momentos en el AAA Bird Shop en la calle Broadway a un lado del AAA Merchant Store de los Archuleta. Vio unos cuantos pájaros en sus perchas en la ventana de la tienda. Unos estaban con su canto o pepenaban semillas y comiéndoselas. Todos con plumajes brillantes y de distintos colores. Quico se puso a pensar. Se rascaba la cabeza. Cuanto más veía aquella escena, más se le metía en la cabeza que a lo mejor un buen regalo, algo inesperado y sorprendente, sería un ave. "Por qué no," se dijo para sí, y entró en el AAA Bird Shop.

—Buenos días—saludo cordial de un hombre alto con bigote—. ¿En qué puedo servirle caballero?

—Pues, no sé exactamente. Tal vez usté pueda ayudarme.

—Con mucho gusto. Yo soy Bonifacio, el dueño. Todos me llaman Boni. Ahora bien, ¿qué se le ofrece?

Quico estuvo explicándole los años que llevaba casado con su esposa y el hecho de que ya estaba cansado de regalarle chocolates y flores para su cumpleaños. Era hora de sorprenderla con algo distinto y original.

—A propósito, ¿cómo se llama usté?—le preguntó Bonifacio.

—Quico. Yo y mi esposa Quica vivimos en el barrio de Santa Bárbara no muy lejos de aquí.

—¡Bingo!—dijo repentinamente— Ya sé que puede regalarle a su querida esposa para su cumpleaños.

—¡No me diga!

—Un perico—le propuso el dueño con una sonrisa irónica—. ¿Qué le parece? Además, perico rima con Quico, je, je—añadió él lo cual le tuvo gracia a Quico—. No solamente eso, tengo un perico que habla. Bueno, por lo menos dice dos o tres palabras. Venga. Se lo enseño. Ahí está. ¿Qué le parece?

El perico era lindo. Tenía plumaje verde y relumbroso. Apenas tenía año y medio de edad según el dueño. También le aseguró a Quico que dentro de poco tiempo el perico sería capaz de aprender más palabras.

—¿Y qué palabras sabes?—le preguntó Quico.

—Te amo—contestó Bonifacio sin hesitar.

—¡Perfecto! Las palabras "te amo" ya lo dicen todo. ¿Y por cuánto me lo vende? Pero no me vaya a cobrar un ojo de la cara—le advirtió Quico en broma.

—No, no, no. Se lo vendo barato. Dos pesos.

—Trato hecho—exclamó Quico, y sacó un billete arrugado de un peso de su bolsa de monedas, y cuatro monedas de dos reales cada una—. Tenga usted—y Bonifacio cogió el perico de la jaula para entregárselo a Quico.

—¿Y el perico pica o no?

—Pues todos los pericos pican. Es parte de su naturaleza. Pican para comer, pican para . . .

—Entonces tendrá que regalarme la jaula—interrumpió Quico—. Si no, devuélvame el dinero porque no puedo soltar el perico en mi taller (Quico tenía fama por sus trabajos de piel.).

—Mire, siendo que usté vive cerca y es vecino, no tiene que darme ni un centavo por la jaula. Hasta le voy a dar un saquito de semillas que le dé de comer. Le durarán unos días.

—Muchísimas gracias. Usté es muy amable.

Quico se marchó contentísimo. Se remudaba la jaula y el perico de una mano a la otra según iba andando para no cansarse. Iba chiflando como un niño mientras caminaba hasta llegar a casa. Ahora venía lo bueno. ¿Cómo entrar en su taller detrás de la casa sin que lo viera o lo oyera Quica? "Menos mal que no tenemos perro," pensó él. Entró de puntillas y colgó la jaula de una viga en su taller.

Salió de su taller calladito y entró en la casa por el portal que daba a la calle Edith Boulevard y al cementerio de Santa Bárbara.

—Amor mío—dijo Quica al verlo—. ¿Por qué te tardaste tanto? Aquí me tenías con la pena—y lo abrazó.

—Pues andando ida y vuelta a pie a la Plaza y con los años que tengo se tarda uno. Al regresar me entretuve con mi amigo David Orozco donde siempre me hacía el pelo.

—¿Quieres un cafecito?

—¡Sí, cómo no!

—Aquí tienes querido, café con leche como te gusta . . . y dos bizcochitos pa que sopees. Acabo de hacerlos—y le plantó un beso a su marido en la frente.

Aún faltaban tres días para el cumpleaños de Quica. Entretanto Quico se pasaba las mañanas en su taller. Él estaba acostumbrado a que su esposa no lo molestara. Así pudo darle de comer al perico y agua sin que ella se diera cuenta. La única cosa es que cada vez que entraba Quico en su taller el perico le repetía, "Te amo. Te amo," lo cual le hacía reír.

Por fin llegó el viernes, el cumpleaños de Quica. Quico además de ser diestro en maniobra de piel, también cocinaba un arroz con pollo sabrosísimo. Es lo que le preparó a su querida esposa para honrar su cumpleaños. De postre hubo unas natillas sabrosas que le trajo una vecina que vivía a un lado.

—Amor, tu arroz con pollo como siempre estuvo para chuparse uno los dedos. Gracias, querido.

—Al contrario. Gracias a ti por ser tan buena esposa a través de los años . . . espérate un momentito. Te tengo una sorpresa—y volvió con la jaula tapada con una vieja camisa azul suya—. ¡Feliz cumpleaños!—proclamó en voz alta Quico—. Aquí tienes—. No acababa de destapar la jaula cuando el perico soltó sus cariñosas palabras. "Te amo. Te amo." Quica se rió. Le tuvo gracia el perico.

—¡Ay Dios mío! Un perico que habla. ¡Qué sorpresa!—y le dio un abrazo fuerte a su marido.

—¿Te gusta?

—Sí, y lo que me agrada más a primera vista son las plumas tan verdes. Me hacen recordar del vestido verde que me regalaste para nuestro décimo aniversario unos años atrás. Todavía lo tengo.

—Bueno, ahora tienes que decidir dónde poner a tu amigo—y se sonrió Quico.

—Pues durante el día lo podemos poner en el portal y por la noche lo metemos en la casa. ¿Qué te parece?

—Bien—dijo Quico—. Ahora viene lo bueno. ¿Qué nombre quieres ponerle al perico? Debe tener nombre. No podemos estar llamándolo perico.

—Ya eso es más difícil. Tendré que pensar en un buen nombre.

Pasaron unos días. Nada le venía a la cabeza a Quica. Se rascaba la cabeza, pero ni la menor idea. Se levantó temprano una mañana al rayar el sol. ¡Zas! "Por qué no ponerle el nombre Sol," se dijo a sí misma.

Quico acababa de levantarse y entró en la cocina medio dormido, refregándose los ojos.

—Buenos días, querido. Más vale tarde que nunca, eh—y le puso una taza de café con leche—. Pues hoy soy yo la que tiene una sorpresa.

—No me digas. ¿Qué sorpresa puede ser a estas horas de la mañana?

—Tengo un nombre para el perico. ¡Sol!

—Ah, me gusta. ¿Y cómo se te ocurrió ese nombre?

—Fue fácil—dijo con una risita—. Al rayar el sol esta mañana pensé en ti, mi amor. Tú eres el sol que brilla en mi vida día tras día. Y no sólo eso, ahora tengo dos amores—tú y Sol. Ustedes dos me dicen "Te amo, te amo." ¿Qué más queda?

Se disculpó Quico y volvió en seguida con Sol y la pajarera y se la entregó a Quica.

—Te amo, te amo—repitió Sol.

—Yo también la amo—añadió Quico. Luego vio a Quica que le escurría una lágrima por cada mejilla.

Mrs. Fortnight

FABIANA AND HER HUSBAND, Olmedo, epitomize the antithesis of Quico and Quica. Mrs. Fortnight, as Fabiana became known in the barrio, and her husband, were very much in love but ultimately they both suffered tragedy and sadness.

Fabiana was a woman of about sixty-odd years old who had eye problems. That's why she wore very thick glasses, which made her face look rounder and older. The story goes that she had lived a long time in Santa Barbara on a backstreet (now called Gómez Avenue) and was known in the neighborhood by the nickname Mrs. Fortnight. No one knows who named her that. To be sure, it was not a show of respect, but let's not get ahead of ourselves. Let us go back in time.

Fabiana's husband, Olmedo, was six or seven years older than she. For many years he was a workman at the Santa Fe Shops, the railyards southeast of Albuquerque. He worked there for a long time until he retired.

One morning as he and his wife were eating breakfast alone, since they didn't have any children, she surprised him.

"Good news, my dear! Starting next week I want to fix for you, at least once a month, one of your favorite dishes. What do you say?"

"Wonderful, but why? To what do I owe all of that?" he asked, a tad confused. "Throughout the years I've never complained about the meals you've cooked for me."

"Look, my love. I wish to do it as a gesture of kindness and appreciation for all the years you worked at the Shops."

"Okay, whatever you say. You're the boss. I'm only the dishwasher," he countered with a smile.

"Now," Fabiana continued, "you'll be able to enjoy your favorite meals more calmly. And as I told you, I want to do this for all the months and weeks that you labored at the Shops. The endless days that you walked to work, both coming and going—in summer as well as in winter—instead of taking the bus just to save money, are also still fresh in my mind. Nobody knows that better than me. And your job was hard and dirty work. I know because I'm the one who washed your grubby shirts and bib overalls covered with grease."

"You're right. And I have never forgotten how spotless I looked when I arrived at the Shops on Monday mornings. My coworkers were in awe. They admired my clean and well-ironed shirts. Why, you even treated my bib overalls to a bit of starch so that they wouldn't wrinkle."

Of course, now that Olmedo was retired, not a day went by that he didn't have a good appetite, especially on weekends. They were like a modest fiesta. Fabiana got up early one Sunday morning. Today for lunch she was going to prepare one of her husband's favorite dishes. She cooked a *caldito* (stew) of cubed pork, boiled potatoes, and green chile (sun-dried). Fried zucchini, roasted corn on the cob, and flat oven bread (*brel*) complemented the caldito.

"Come, my dear. Time to eat," she said, and he sat at the table. "I bet you can't guess what I have for you today," and she uncovered the pan of caldito. He sprung to his feet and gave his wife a hearty hug.

Olmedo was a good eater. He ate with gusto and relished each bite. Even tiny droplets of perspiration dripped from his forehead.

For dessert Fabiana served him lemon meringue pie that she had just taken out of the oven. Olmedo was in seventh heaven. He looked at her from across the table and blew her a kiss.

"I ate like a glutton," declared Olmedo with a wry smile, as he rubbed his stomach. Fabiana looked at him. She felt great joy in her heart.

Within time, Olmedo gained more and more weight. Neither he nor his wife noticed his obesity. Sooner or later his health began to worry her. All the same, Fabiana, as usual, continued to get up early on weekends to brew coffee to take to her husband in bed. The Saturday before Palm Sunday she entered the bedroom to see if he was awake, but he didn't move. She shook him but nothing happened. She got frightened and thought he was dead. Then she saw his enormous belly moving slowly up and down. She felt tremendous relief. She shook him again.

"What? What? What happened? Am I late for work?" He reacted half dazed and was beside himself.

"Calm down! Calm down!" Fabiana begged him. "It was nothing. Just a nightmare. Lean up against the bed. I'll bring your coffee and milk right away."

She quickly returned with the coffee and milk and two bizcochitos. He loved to dunk them even though he never failed to leave half of the bizcochitos in the bottom of the cup. But he quickly spooned the crumbs out with a teaspoon. Nothing was lost.

"I'll be right back. I'm going to feed the stove a log," said Fabiana.

She returned. She quickly noticed that her husband had not sipped a drop of coffee. She became worried.

"My God! What's happening to you?" she exclaimed in a worried voice.

"Nothing, nothing. Why do you ask?" he responded, a bit impatient.

"Look at your face. You're as pale as that bedsheet. Tell me, do you feel sick? And don't lie to me," she said, and she hugged him.

"The truth is, I don't know what's wrong with me. Last night I was awake and couldn't sleep, practically all night long. I even had difficulty breathing. I felt anxiety. I got desperate. A scary thing."

"I think it's good for a doctor to come see you. We'll see what he says."

Next day, Dr. Wilder came. He examined Olmedo. The preliminary news was not encouraging.

"Don Olmedo, the reason you have trouble breathing is because of your heart. It skips, and at times speeds up. I see that you are quite heavy and perhaps that's part of the problem. I advise you to come to my office for more tests," and the doctor bid him a cordial good-bye.

"I'm not going to any pig's dirty office. The only thing doctors want is to suck money out of you," shouted Olmedo. "He can go to hell, along with the rest of the bloodsuckers. End of story."

Fabiana was stunned. For a few brief moments she was speechless. Finally a few words came to her.

"I believe it's me who's to blame. From this day forward I will quit fixing you your favorite dishes. Surely they are to blame for your physical discomfort."

"Don't come to me with that nonsense," reacted Olmedo rather impatiently. "You have treated me as though I were a child, and with much kindness. I shall never forget that."

His wife pretended to listen but his words went in one ear and out the other. Her distress regarding her husband's health persisted, and day after day he continued to act weirdly. The words and phrases that came out of his mouth at times didn't make any sense.

Fabiana, too, started to act in a rather outlandish manner. The fifteenth of the month came, as well as her husband's pension check. Instead of going to the grocery store to cash the check and do her shopping as usual, she sneaked out of the house while her husband rested. For the first time ever she visited Beba Usted, a liquor store on Edith Boulevard and Mountain Road. She went in and walked up one aisle and down another, eyeing a stream of bottles.

"Good morning, ma'am," said a cordial man with an enormous belly that made Fabiana think of her husband. "What can I do for you?"

"I would like a jug of muscatel," she said—a name that she was acquainted with because years back she had a neighbor who drank that brand of wine.

"I'm sorry lady, but it only comes in bottles," and he showed her one.

"How much is it?"

"It's cheap. Four bits (50 cents) per bottle."

"Very well. But can you cash my husband's pension check? He's already endorsed it."

"Let me see it. Ah, your husband worked at the Santa Fe Shops. I'll cash it. Why not."

"Okay, I'll take two bottles of muscatel," and she paid him. "But please wrap them up for me."

She reached home a little before noon. She went into the kitchen but didn't see her husband where he usually rested. She quickly hid the wine in the cupboard so that he didn't see it and then went to look for him. He was lying on the living room floor, motionless.

"Dear! Dear! Move! What's wrong with you?" She shook him. She then saw that his eyes rolled. She was terrified.

Fabiana ran to tell Jesusita, her good neighbor whose son had a car. With the help of the son, the two women lifted Olmedo with some difficulty but managed to load him into the car, and they headed for the hospital. As they arrived at Saint Joseph's Hospital in Martíneztown, Olmedo started to grumble and to move a bit before the nurses took him on a stretcher to the emergency room.

Fabiana waited and waited. She became anxious. Finally the doctor walked into the waiting room and introduced himself. Before he could tell her the bad news she stood up.

"Doctor, doctor, how is my husband?"

"Sit down, please sit down. We have run several tests and your husband has suffered a serious stroke. He's going to need a lot of assistance."

"Like what?" Fabiana asked desperately.

"Professional care. I recommend that you take your husband to the Nazareth Sanatorium in Los Ranchos de Alburquerque. He'll be in good hands."

"Thank you very much," said Fabiana, in a disconsolate mood. "May I see my husband now?" And the doctor escorted her to Olmedo's room. She went in, saw him, and caressed his forehead, but he didn't react. He didn't even open his eyes. Fabiana started sobbing. Tears trickled down her face. She felt enormous pain.

Jesusita and her son took Fabiana home. The first thing she did was to fetch a bottle of wine from the cupboard and start drinking. She took sip after sip until she finished first one whole bottle, and then the second one. Next day she woke up, half drunk, with a headache. She heard knocks on the kitchen door but paid no attention.

"Neighbor, neighbor! It's me, Jesusita. I came to see how you're doing." She found her sitting on the bed with empty bottles of wine on the small table next to the bed. "How are you feeling?"

"Well, for whatever ails you, there's nothing better than good muscatel," she responded in a brusque and ironic manner.

Three days elapsed before Fabiana returned to the hospital. She made arrangements to transfer her husband to the Nazareth Sanatorium, just as the doctor had recommended. She would thus be able to visit him anytime—at least three times per week. Soon she realized that Olmedo barely spoke. And what he said didn't make much sense. He seemed to be in a distant world.

Fabiana, from one day to the next, became more and more disillusioned. She missed her beloved husband. His absence left a painful void at home and in her heart. The visitations to the sanatorium were of little consolation. The more she missed him, the more wine she drank. Her first purchases, every two weeks after she received her husband's pension check, were at the Beba Usted liquor store. But now instead of buying one or two bottles of wine, she bought three or four. On weekends she drank bottle after bottle as though it were water.

One Sunday morning after Mass, Mom asked me to pump some water from my grandparents' well to brew coffee for Dad. Suddenly

I saw this woman, practically nude, shouting in the street, but you couldn't understand what she was saying. I took off running to tell Mom.

"Mom! Mom!" I said, as I dashed inside our little house.

"What, hijito? How come you dashed in here like a bolt of lightning?"

"You're not going to believe this. There's this woman in the street, almost stark naked. And she screams and screams as though she's crying. I'm going to see Grandma Lale. She must know who she is," and I ran next door to see her.

"Oh, hijito. She's a woman who lives nearby. Her name is Fabiana, but some people call her Mrs. Fortnight."

"Why, Grandma?"

"Because she drinks a lot of wine—above all, every fifteen days when she gets her husband's check. That's when she goes out into the street drunk and shouts nonsense since she misses her husband, who's at a sanatorium."

Within time I saw that Mrs. Fortnight went out into the street dead drunk, staggering, barefoot, and with nothing on except her underskirt. She shouted and shouted endless nonsense and bad words. The neighbors who heard her discordant voice pried open their windows to see who it was, although they suspected that it was Fabiana, that is, Mrs. Fortnight. Some women were shocked but at the same time felt sorry for her.

The poor soul went from bad to worse. Her appetite for food—and sleep—came and went in spurts. And she hardly ever combed her hair or washed up. Not having Olmedo at home was killing her. She was dying of loneliness.

In a given moment of tranquility and lucidity, she decided to give up drinking. It also got into her head to sell the house and to go live at the Nazareth Sanatorium to be closer to her husband. She could then see him more frequently. "Whether you like it or not, my love, here I am," she said to herself.

She soon realized that he remained in another world. There

were no chitchats, jokes—nothing—only the touching of hands and a hug now and then. She was close to her husband, of course, but at the same time far away from him. Any sense of closeness stemmed from the soaked handkerchiefs from crying every time she saw her beloved husband. She continued to blame herself for the very good meals she had fed him throughout the years.

Fabiana and Olmedo continued living at the Nazareth Sanatorium but were worlds apart emotionally. Even her good neighbor Jesusita, who went to visit Fabiana sooner or later, became disenchanted and quit going to spend moments with her.

"Neighbor," she said to Fabiana in a sad and pensive tone the last time she went to see her, "in this world there is no pain that the soul cannot bear," and Jesusita bid her good-bye.

Two weeks went by and Jesusita could not resist the temptation to visit her friend. When she stepped inside the foyer of the sanatorium the first thing she saw was the bulletin board: Fabiana and Olmedo Passed Away. Overcome with tremendous sadness, she sat down and thought of her friend. Out of the blue these words came to her lips.

Mi querida Fabiana,
aunque te has ido,
ahora están juntitos
para siempre
tú y tu marido.
///
My dear Fabiana,
though you are gone,
now you and your husband
are happily together
for ever and ever.
R.I.P.

La Señora Quincena

FABIANA Y SU ESPOSO Olmedo personifican lo opuesto de Quico y Quica. La Sra. Quincena, pues así llegó a conocerse Fabiana en el barrio, y su esposo estaban muy enamorados pero al fin y al cabo ambos sufrieron tristeza y tragedia.

Fabiana era una señora de unos sesenta años y pico que padecía de la vista. Por eso usaba unos anteojos bastante gruesos los cuales le hacían la cara más redonda y vieja. Se dice que había vivido por mucho tiempo en una calle secundaria en Santa Bárbara (hoy en día se llama Gómez Avenue) y se conocía por el apodo Sra. Quincena. No se sabe quién le puso ese sobrenombre. De hecho no era señal de respeto, pero no nos adelantemos. Demos un vistazo hacia el pasado.

El esposo de Fabiana era seis o siete años mayor que ella. Por muchos años fue obrero en los Shapes de Santa Fe, la estación de ferrocarril al suroeste de Alburquerque. Allí trabajó por mucho tiempo hasta que se jubiló.

Una mañana mientras él y su esposa desayunaban solitos, ya que no tenían hijos, lo sorprendió ella.

—¡Albricias querido! Empezando con la semana que entra quiero prepararte por lo menos una vez al mes uno de tus platos favoritos. ¿Qué te parece?

—Estupendo, ¿pero por qué? ¿A qué debo todo eso?—preguntó él un poco confuso. A través de los años nunca me he quejado de lo que me has cocinado.

—Mira, mi amor. Quiero hacerlo como gesto de cariño y agradecimiento por todos los años que trabajaste en los Shapes.

—Bueno, como tú digas. Tú eres la jefa. Yo apenas soy el lavaplatos—respondió él sonriendo.

—Ahora—continuó Fabiana—, podrás gozar de tus comidas favoritas con más calma. Y como te dije, quiero hacerlo por toditos los meses y las semanas que trabajaste en los Shapes. El sin fin de días que fuiste a pie a trabajar, tanto yendo como viniendo, en verano e invierno, para ahorrar dinero en vez de tomar el bos aún están frescos en mi mente. Nadie sabe eso mejor que yo. Y tu trabajo fue pesado y sucio. Yo sé porque fui la que te lavó las camisas y las pecheras roñosas empapadas de unto.

—Dices bien, y a mí nunca se me olvida lo limpio que llegaba yo a los Shapes los lunes por la mañana. Mis compañeros se quedaban con la boca abierta. Admiraban mi camisa limpia y bien planchada. Hasta mis pecheras les ponías tú un poco de almidón para que no se arrugaran.

Claro está que ahora Olmedo estando jubilado no había días que le faltara su buen apetito, en particular los fines de semana. Eran como una pequeña fiesta. Un domingo se levantó temprano Fabiana. Hoy para el lonche le iba a preparar a su esposo uno de los platos favoritos de él. Le guisó un caldito con carne de cerdo, patatas cocidas, y chile verde seco. Incluso le puso calabacitas fritas, maíz en elote tostado, y brel para acompañar el caldito.

—Anda querido mío. Es hora de comer—y se sentó él a la mesa—. A que no sabes qué te tengo hoy—y destapó la olla con el caldito. Saltó y se puso de pie y le dio un fuerte abrazo a su esposa.

Olmedo era buen comedor. Comía con ánimo y saboreaba cada bocado. Hasta le escurrían gotitas de sudor en la frente.

De postre le puso Fabiana pastel de limón bien calentito que apenas acababa de sacar del horno de la estufa. Olmedo estaba por los cielos. La miró él desde el otro lado de la mesa y le tiró un beso.

—Comí como un barril sin fondo—declaró Olmedo con una

risita palpándose el estómago. Fabiana lo miró. Sintió un gusto tremendo en su corazón.

Con el tiempo Olmedo fue engordando cada vez más. Ni él ni su esposa se dieron cuenta de su gordura. Tarde o temprano su salud empezó a preocuparle a ella.

Fabiana como de costumbre seguía levantándose temprano los fines de semana para hacer café y llevarle a su esposo en cama. Un sábado antes del Domingo de Ramos ella entró en el cuarto de dormir para ver si él estaba despierto, pero no se movía. Ella lo sacudió pero nada. Se espantó y creyó que estaba muerto. Luego vio que su enorme panza se movía despacito para arriba y para abajo. Sintió un alivio tremendo ella. Volvió a sacudirlo.

—¿Qué? ¿Qué? ¿Qué pasó? ¿Ya voy tarde al trabajo?—reaccionó medio aturdido y fuera de sí.

—¡Cálmate! ¡Cálmate!—le suplicó Fabiana—. No fue nada. Nada más que una pesadilla. Respáldate contra la cama. En seguida te traigo tu café con leche.

Pronto regresó con el café con leche y dos bizcochitos. A él le gustaba sopearlos aunque siempre solía dejar la mitad de los bizcochitos en el fondo de la taza. Pero pronto sacaba las migajas con una cucharita. No se perdía nada.

—Ya vuelvo. Voy a echarle un leño a la estufa—dijo Fabiana.

Volvió ella. Pronto se dio cuenta que su marido no había bebido ni una gota del café. Le dio pena.

—¡Dios mío! ¿Qué te pasa?—exclamó en una voz inquietante.

—Nada, nada. ¿Por qué preguntas?—respondió él un poco impaciente.

—Mira como tienes la cara. Estás tan pálido como esa sábana. Dime, ¿te sientes mal? Y no me mientas—y lo abrazó.

—La verdad es que no sé qué me pasa. Anoche se me espantó el sueño y no pude dormir casi la noche entera. Hasta ni siquiera alcanzaba resuello. Me daban ansias. Me desesperaba. Cosa fea.

—Yo creo que es bueno que venga un doctor a verte. Ya veremos qué dice él—.

Al día siguiente vino el Dr. Wilder. Examinó a Olmedo. Las noticias preliminares no fueron buenas.

—Don Olmedo, la razón por la cual usted tiene problemas respirando es que padece del corazón. Da saltos y a veces se acelera. Veo que usted pesa bastante y tal vez eso sea parte del problema. Le aconsejo que venga a mi oficina para más exámenes—y se despidió cordialmente el médico.

—Yo no voy a ninguna oficina de estos marranos. Lo único que quieren los doctores es sacarle a uno dinero—vociferó Olmedo—. Que se vaya al infierno con todos los demás chupasangres. Se acabó.

Fabiana se quedó atónita. Por unos breves momentos no supo qué decir. Por fin le vinieron unas cuantas palabras.

—Creo que soy yo la que tiene la culpa. Desde hoy en adelante dejo de cocinarte tus platos favoritos. Sin duda que han contribuido a tu malestar físico.

—No me vengas con esas tonterías—reaccionó Olmedo de una manera impaciente—. Tú me has tratado como si yo fuera un niño y con mucho cariño. Nunca se me olvidará eso.

Su esposa se hacía como que le escuchaba pero sus palabras le entraron por un oído y le salieron por el otro. Su desconsuelo tocante a la salud de su marido persistía, y día tras día él seguía portándose de una manera muy extraña. Las palabras y frases que escupía a veces no tenían sentido.

Fabiana también empezó a portarse de una manera estrambótica. Llegó el día quince del mes junto con el cheque de pensión de su marido. En vez de ir a la tienda de comestibles para cambiar el cheque y hacer sus compras como de costumbre, se escabulló de casa mientras su esposo descansaba. Se fue por primera vez en su vida a la licorería Beba Usted en la calle Edith cerca de Mountain Road. Entró. Se paseaba por un pasillo y luego por otro, ojeando un chorro de botellas.

—Buenos días, señora—saludo cordial de un hombre con una barriga enorme que le hizo pensar a Fabiana en Olmedo—. ¿En qué puedo servirle?

—Quisiera una botija de Moscatel—nombre que ella conocía porque tuvo un vecino años atrás que tomaba esa marca de vino.

—Lo siento señora, pero solamente viene en botellas—y le enseñó una.

—¿Cuánto es?

—Es barato. Cuatro reales por botella.

—Está bien. ¿Pero me puede cambiar el cheque de pensión de mi marido? Ya lo firmó él.

—Déjeme verlo. Ah, su esposo trabajó en los Shapes de Santa Fe. Se lo cambio. Por qué no.

—Pues bien. Me llevo dos botellas de Moscatel—y le pagó—. Pero envuélvamelas por favor.

Llegó a casa poco antes del mediodía. Entró en la cocina pero no vio a su esposo donde acostumbraba descansar. Pronto escondió el vino en el trastero para que no lo viera él y luego se fue a buscarlo. Lo encontró en el suelo en la sala de estar. No se movía.

—¡Querido! ¡Querido! ¡Muévete! ¿Qué tienes?—. Lo sacudió. Luego vio que tenía los ojos en blanco. Le entró un miedo espantoso.

Fabiana partió corriendo a avisarle a Jesusita, su buena vecina cuyo hijo tenía carro. Con la ayuda del hijo y las dos mujeres levantaron a Olmedo a duras penas pero pudieron echarlo en el coche y se fueron al hospital. Al llegar al Hospital San José en Martíneztown empezó a refunfuñar y a moverse un poco antes de llevarlo las enfermeras en una camilla de ruedas a la sala de emergencia.

Fabiana esperaba y esperaba. Le daban ansias. Por fin entró el médico en la sala de espera y se presentó. Antes de que pudiera comunicarle las malas noticias, se puso ella de pie.

—Doctor, doctor, ¿cómo está mi marido?

—Siéntese, siéntese por favor. Hemos hechos varios exámenes y su marido ha sufrido un ataque cerebral bastante serio. Va necesitar mucha ayuda.

—¿Cómo qué?—preguntó Fabiana exasperada.

—Asistencia profesional. Yo le recomiendo que lleve a su esposo al Sanatorio Nazareno en los Ranchos de Alburquerque. Estará en buenas manos.

—Muchas gracias—dijo Fabiana bien desconsolada—. ¿Puedo ver a mi esposo ahora?—y la acompañó el médico al cuarto de Olmedo. Entró, lo vio, y le acarició la frente, pero él no reaccionó. Ni siquiera abrió los ojos. Fabiana empezó a sollozar. Le escurrían chorros de lágrimas. Sintió un dolor enorme.

Jesusita y su hijo la llevaron a casa. Lo primero que hizo Fabiana fue sacar una botella de vino del trastero y se puso a tomar. Tomó sorbo tras sorbo hasta que se acabó primero una botella entera y después la segunda. Al día siguiente despertó con dolores de cabeza y media borracha. Oyó toques en la puerta de la cocina pero no hizo caso.

—¡Vecina, vecina! Soy yo, Jesusita. Vine a ver cómo sigue—. La halló sentada en la cama con botellas vacías de vino en la mesita al lado de la cama. —¿Cómo se siente?

—Pues para todo buen mal no hay nada como un buen mescal—contestó de una manera tosca e irónica.

Tres días transcurrieron antes de regresar Fabiana al hospital. Hizo arreglos para que transportaran a su esposo al Sanatorio Nazareno, tal y como había recomendado el médico. Así podría ella visitarlo a cualquier hora por lo menos tres veces por semana. No tardó en darse cuenta de que Olmedo apenas hablaba. Y lo que decía no tenía mucho sentido. Parecía estar en un mundo lejano.

Fabiana de un día a otro se desanimaba más y más. Echaba de menos a su querido marido. Su ausencia había dejado un hueco doloroso en casa y en su corazón. Las visitas al sanatorio eran de poco consuelo. Mientras más lo extrañaba, más vino tomaba. Sus primeras compras cada quincena al recibir el cheque de pensión de su marido eran en la licorería Beba Usted. Pero ahora en vez de comprarse una o dos botellas de vino, se compraba tres o cuatro. Los fines de semana se empinaba las botellas como si fueran agua.

Un domingo por la mañana después de misa, me mandó mamá a

que sacara agua de la noria que tenían mis abuelitos para prepararle café a papá. De repente vi a esta mujer casi desnuda en la calle gritando en voz alta, pero no se le entendía lo que decía. Salí corriendo a avisarle a mamá.

—¡Amá, amá!—le dije al entrar de vuelo en nuestra casita.

—¿Qué hijito? ¡Qué relámpago ni qué nada!

—No lo vas a creer. Anda esta mujer en la calle casi en pelota. Y grita y grita como que llora. Voy a ver a mi agüelita Lale. Ella debe saber quién es—y me fui corriendo a verla.

—Oh, hijito. Es una mujer que vive cerquita. Se llama Fabiana, pero algunas gentes la llaman la Sra. Quincena.

—¿Por qué agüelita?

—Porque toma demasiado vino sobre todo cada quince días cuando le llega el cheque de su marido. Es cuando sale a la calle borracha y grita disparates siendo que echa de menos a su marido que está en un sanatorio.

Con el tiempo vi que la Sra. Quincena salía tambaleando a la calle bien emborrachada, descalza, y con nada más que su enagua. Gritaba y gritaba un sin fin de disparates y palabrotas. Los vecinos que oían aquella voz discordante abrían las ventanas para ver quién era aunque sospechaban que era Fabiana, o sea, la Sra. Quincena. Algunas mujeres se quedaban espantadas pero a la misma vez les daba lástima.

La pobrecita fue de mal en peor. Lo poco que comía—o dormía—era a brincos y a saltos. Y casi nunca se peinaba o se lavaba. No tener a Olmedo en casa la estaba matando. Se moría de tristeza.

En un dado momento de tranquilidad y lucidez, decidió dejar la botella. De igual forma se le metió en la cabeza vender la casa e irse a vivir en el Sanatorio Nazareno para estar cerca de su esposo. Así podría verlo más a menudo. "Por las buenas o por las malas, amor mío, aquí me tienes," dijo ella para sí.

Pronto se dio cuenta que él persistía en otro mundo No había pláticas, chistes, nada, sólo toques de mano y uno que otro abrazo. Estaba cerca de su marido, claro, pero a la misma vez bien lejos de él. Cualquier sentido de intimidad partía de sus paños empapados de lágrimas cada vez que veía a su querido marido. Ella seguía echándose la culpa a sí misma por todas las buenas comidas que le dio de comer a través de los años.

Fabiana y Olmedo siguieron viviendo en el Sanatorio Nazareno pero mundos aparte emotivamente. Hasta su buena vecina Jesusita que iba a visitar a Fabiana, tarde o temprano se desanimó y dejó de ir a pasar sus ratos con ella.

—Vecina—le dijo a Fabiana en un tono triste y pensativo la última vez que fue a verla—, en este mundo no hay dolor que el alma no aguante—y se despidió de ella Jesusita.

Pasaron dos semanas y Jesusita no podía resistir la tentación de visitar a su amiga. Cuando entró en el vestíbulo del sanatorio lo primero que vio fue el tablón de anuncios: Fabiana y Olmedo Muertos. Acogida por una tristeza enorme, se sentó y pensó en su amiga. De la nada le vinieron estas palabras a sus labios.

Mi querida Fabiana,
aunque te has ido,
ahora están juntitos
para siempre
tú y tu marido.
Q. E. P. D.

The Man Who Swore a Lot

GRANDMA LALE, MY COUSIN Rita Ruelas, and I were on our way home from the Felipe García's store when we heard a voice. At first I thought it was Fabiana spewing her nonsense, but it quickly dawned on me that she was dead. It also wasn't clear which one of the two alleys the voice was coming from, but as we walked, we realized that it was a man's harsh voice, which grew louder and louder.

As I looked toward the right, I saw this bearded gentleman wearing a squashed hat, tilted to one side. He was leaning up against the wall of Las Chanclas Tavern.

"Look, Grandma! What's that man doing?" I asked.

"Junie, he's urinating," she exclaimed, rather annoyed. "He's probably drunk," she added.

While the man took care of business he cursed and insulted those whose steps and voices he heard behind him. You could tell from his vulgar language that he had had more than a few drinks the night before.

"I crap all over every SOB who may be listening or who's seeing me irrigate this fine wall. No one in this lousy world, in this forsaken neighborhood, takes pity on a drunkard like me. All you drooling idiots are nothing more than a bunch of shameless scoundrels. Spongers, all of you! And if someone doesn't like what I say let him eat *mierda* (shit). Or let him stick his finger where it's convenient (where the sun doesn't shine) to lower the fever so he can feel better."

"Come hijitos, my children. Let's go, quickly. Don't pay attention to that dirty, filthy pig. Everything he says makes no sense at all; that's drunks for you. That man is always mouthing off, above all when he's drunk."

"Who is he, Grandma? What's wrong with him? How come he looks so dirty?" Rita asked.

"His name is Tranquilino, the Tank. That's what he's called because he drinks a lot. He lost his marbles many years ago."

"Where did he lose them, Grandma?" I asked innocently, but my grandma barely paid attention to the question. She was more preoccupied by what Rita and I had seen and heard.

"But what happened to the marbles?" I asked once again.

"What? Who? What is it, my child?" Grandma asked, a tad distracted, while paying more attention to Tranquilino's craziness.

"I asked what happened to his marbles."

"No, no. That's not what it means. Look, it has nothing to do with marbles. That's what we say when someone has lost a nut and a screw."

"But why do you say that he's lost a nut and a . . . ?"

"Because Tranquilino has lost his mind. He no longer whistles a pretty tune the way he once did. But look, we're all a little bit crazy in the head, like an overly wound-up clock. Do you understand?"

I could only scratch my head. I didn't try to make heads or tails out of Grandma's string of gobbledygook.

"Is it the same thing as saying he's got a few loose screws?" Rita asked.

"That's it, hijita! Now you've hit the nail on the head. That's what's wrong with Tranquilino. He's nuts. He lost a screw. He's gone bananas. His head is full of wasps."

Just then Grandma Lale saw two neighbors coming down the street raising a cloud of dust. They were in a big hurry.

"May God greet you a good morning, neighbor," said Francisquita to Grandma Lale. "How are you?"

"Very, very well, thanks be to God. And you?" Grandma asked.

"Getting by. We're in a hurry to mail my daughter this letter at the post office. I want it to leave this morning."

Before reaching the post office Francisquita and her friend Sofía heard the same voice as Grandma Lale, Rita, and me. Tranquilino was still spewing his string of nonsense and bad words.

"Ladies, where are you going in such a hurry, as though you had a corn cob up your ass? You're just like all the other old widowed hags. You can't sit still. Always acting like a bunch of moody hens. You spend all your time looking for a log (penis) to stick in your fireplace (to have sex). You're never at a loss to find a good-looking stud to have sex with. All you do is screw around to see who can rock you in bed. Nothing but hump, hump."

"My goodness, comadre!" said Sofía. "Is that the same mouth that man eats with?"

"Don't pay any attention to him. Tranquilino's been an orphan all his life. He respects no one. The son of a whore doesn't even know who his mother is. And his father who stuck his wedge in a stranger's nook—nobody knows who he is either."

"If your husbands, who are in heaven, knew the filth you're involved in, they would beg my Father Almighty to send you to hell along with all the other bitches. Your breasts that your lovers suck deserve to dry up for you pretending to be so saintly. And your lovers—they're nothing but a string of motherless creeps, each one strung together waiting his turn to please you. They're nothing but starving dogs that spend all their time looking for a *bizcocho* (female organ) on which to sprinkle cinnamon (to have sex with)."

"Shake a leg, comadre," said Francisquita. "Quickly, before he gets on my nerves and I give him a good whack in the snout. He's foul-mouthed. All he does is swear, spew insults, badmouth, revile, offend, excoriate, imprecate, and censure women. You mark my words: one of these days someone is going to teach him a good lesson."

"You're right, comadre," added Sofía. "For now, he can go screw himself. Let him wallow in his own crap. Never in my lifetime have

I heard a man with such a foul mouth. All he does is cuss. What a disgrace!"

"Come, come, you sodomized and spoiled, rotten women. Here's your little doll that you can play with," continued Tranquilino as the two comadres picked up the pace. "Here's your chile that you can roast."

He tried to follow them, but his legs locked, and he limped. Right then, Tranquilino saw a girl and her mom. His eyes lit up.

"My, what nice thighs just for someone else to caress and enjoy," he said, as he saw the young girl pass by. "Here I'm left like a hot pan and an empty plate with spoon in hand (sexually aroused). Here I'm left with my finger stuck in my mouth, salivating."

"Suck on it until it dries up, you dirty, lousy, and disgusting old man," said a very furious mother.

"Listen here, woman. One doesn't have to look at oneself in the mirror to see an idiot. You're proof of that. It's your beautiful daughter I admire instantly, not you, you fat, flabby ass. Besides, be aware that sooner or later the girl who wishes for a prick can get it from either a poor boy or a rich man."

"You roving, dirty old man. I hope your tongue gets all twisted for being so crude," muttered the mother. Just then she saw Tranquilino out of the corner of one eye giving her the middle finger.

"Come, hijita,"and she grabbed her by the hand, rounded the corner of the alley, and headed home.

Tranquilino then started to sing, in a hoarse and almost inaudible voice, the following verse.

Colorín,
colorete.
Venga pacá,
señora y le pico
l'ojete.
///
Bright rouge,

red as can be.
Come here,
lady, and I'll prick
you with my stick.

He had barely finished his ditty when he lay face down on top of a bench nearby to fall asleep.

In the distance, *rancheras*, Mexican folk music, could be heard coming from Las Chanclas. Closer to him he heard women's voices. Francisquita and her comadre were on their way back from the post office when Francisquita saw Tranquilino on the bench.

"Come, come. Follow me," she said to her comadre Sofía. Then the two tiptoed toward Tranquilino.

"What are you going to do?" her comadre asked.

"I have something nice for Tranquilino that I bought when we stopped at don Felipe's store," her comadre responded with a twinkle in her eye.

"Tranqui, Tranqui," she said, as she tapped him on his shoulder.

"What? What? Who is it?" he reacted, as he rubbed his eyes.

"I have something sweet for you," and she handed him a piece of *piloncillo*, a tasty cone of brown sugar. "Taste it. You'll like it," and Tranquilino took two quick bites. You could tell he was hungry.

"Ummmm. It's delicious," he stated, and chewed as he fell asleep.

"Comadre, what did you give him?"

"It's his dessert," answered Francisquita with a wry smile. "It will give him *pujos*, that is, intestinal cramps and diarrhea to clean his system as well as his mouth."

"My goodness, comadre! Where did you learn all that stuff?"

"Didn't you know I used to be a *curandera* (a healer)?" she remarked sheepishly.

The longer I lived in the Santa Barbara/Martíneztown neighborhood, the more surprises came my way.

El hombre que renegaba mucho

ABUELITA LALE, MI PRIMA Rita Ruelas, y yo regresábamos a casa de la tienda Felipe García cuando oímos una voz. Al principio creí que era Fabiana escupiendo sus disparates, pero bien pronto me di cuenta que ella estaba muerta. Tampoco se sabía de cuál de los dos callejones venía la voz. Según fuimos andando nos dimos cuenta que era la voz ronca de un hombre que se oía cada vez más fuerte.

Al dar yo un vistazo hacia la derecha, vi a este señor barbudo con un sombrero apachurrado, tanteado a un lado. Estaba atrincado contra la pared de la cantina Las Chanclas.

—¡Mire, agüelita! ¿Qué está haciendo ese hombre?—le pregunté.

—Junie—exclamó ella algo molesta—. Está meándose. Tal vez anda borracho.

Mientras el hombre hacía sus necesidades le echaba maldiciones e injuriaba a todos cuyos pasos y voces oía detrás de él. Se notaba por su mala lengua que había tomado más de sus copas la noche anterior.

—Me cago en todo el hijo de puta que me escuche mientras riego esta pader fina. Naide en este pinche mundo, en este barrio desgraciao se conduele de un borracho como yo. Todos ustedes babosos no son más que una bola de cabrones sinvergüenzas.

¡Mantenidos todos! Y si hay alguien a quien no le guste lo que digo, que coma mierda. O que se meta el dedo donde le convenga pa que se le baje la calentura y se sienta mejor.

—Anden, hijitos. Vámonos, pronto. No le hagan caso a ese puerco, cochino. Todo lo que dice no tiene ton ni son; asina son los borrachos. Ese hombre siempre anda disparatando, peor cuando anda borracho.

—¿Quién es, agüelita? ¿Qué le pasa? ¿Por qué anda too roñoso?—preguntó Rita.

—Se llama Tranquilino, el Tanque. Asina le llaman porque toma muncho. Hace munchos años que se le fueron las cabras.

—¿A dónde se le fueron, agüelita?—le pregunté de una manera inocente, pero ella apenas hizo caso a la pregunta. Ella estaba más preocupada por lo que yo y Rita vimos y oímos.

—¿Pero qué pasó con las cabras?—volví a preguntarle.

—¿Qué? ¿Quién? ¿Qué dices, hijito?—preguntó la abuela algo despistada mientras ponía más atención a los disparates de Tranquilino.

—Que si qué pasó con las cabras.

—No, no. No es eso. Mira, no tiene naa que ver con cabras. Eso decimos cuando a alguien le falta una tuerca y un tornillo.

—¿Pero por qué se dice que le hacen falta una tuerca y un . . . ?

—Porque a Tranquilino se le ha ido el juicio. Ya no chifla como chiflaba. Pero mira, a todos se nos suelta la cuerda de vez en cuando lo mesmo que a un reloj. ¿Me entiendes?

Apenas me rascaba la cabeza sin saber lo que significaba todo aquel chorro de palabras de mi abuelita.

—¿Es lo mesmo que decir que tiene unos tornillos sueltos?—preguntó Rita.

—¡Eso es, hijita! Ora sí que tú le atinates. Es lo que tiene Tranquilino. Está zafao. Se le zafó un tornillo. Se le jue la mente pal carajo. Tiene la güeja toa llena de avispas.

En eso vio Abuelita Lale a dos vecinas que venían andando por la calle, levantando una nube de polvo. Andaban apuradas.

—Güenos días le dé Dios, vecina—dijo Francisquita a abuelita Lale—. ¿Cómo amaneció?

—Bien, bien, gracias a Dios. ¿Y usté?—preguntó mi abuelita.

—Aquí nomás. Vamos apuradas a echar esta carta en la estafeta pa mi hija. Quiero que salga esta mañana.

Antes de llegar a correos Francisquita y su amiga Sofía oyeron la misma voz como yo, Abuelita Lale, y Rita. Tranquilino seguía escupiendo su chorro de tonterías y palabrotas.

—¿A dónde van señoras con tanto apuro como si tuvieran un elolote en el fundillo? Ustedes son como toas las otras viudas alcahuetas. No les cabe un güevo en la rosca. Siempre alborotadas como unas gallinas culecas. Se la pasan buscando tronco pa meter en el fogón. No les faltan pencos lechudos pa que les echen un palo. No andan más que puteando pa ver quién las camaltea. Es puro cochar y cochar.

—¡Ay Dios mío, comadre!—dijo Sofía—. ¿Qué con esa boca come ese hombre?

—No le haga caso. Tranquilino ha sido huérfano toda su vida. No le tiene respeto a naiden. El hijo de puta no sabe ni quién es su madre. Y su padre que metió cuña en verija ajena, tampoco se sabe quién es.

—Si sus maridos que están en la gloria supieron de las cochinadas que hacen ustedes, le rogarían ellos a mi Tatita Dios que las mandara a ustedes al infierno con todas las otras perras. Sus chiches que maman sus amantes merecen que se les sequen por creerse ustedes tan santitas. Y sus amantes no son nada más que un chorro de pencos, cada uno encadenao aguardando su turno pa complacerlas a ustedes. Ellos no son más que unos chulos muertos de hambre que se la pasan buscando bizcocho pa salpicarle canela.

—Métale chancla, comadre—dijo Francisquita—. Pronto, antes que se me caliente el casco y le dé un buen fregazo en la trompa. Es un deslenguado. No hace más que puro jurar, insultar, maldecir, injuriar, ofender, execrar, imprecar y vituperar a las mujeres.

Recuerde lo que le digo. Uno de estos días alguien le va a dar una buena lección.

—Dice bien, comadre—añadió Sofía—. Por ahora, que se joda. Ahi que se quede haciendo chile con la rosca. Nunca en mi vida he oído a un hombre con tan mala lengua. Es un puro renegar. ¡Qué bajeza!

—Vengan, vengan mujeres enculadas, malcornadas. Aquí tengo su muñequita pa que jueguen con ella—continuó Tranquilino al acelerar las dos comadres el paso—. Aquí tienen su chile pa rescoldar.

Quiso seguirlas él, pero se le trabaron las piernas y cojeaba. En eso vio venir Tranquilino a una muchacha con su mamá. Se le abrieron los ojos bien grandes.

—¡Ay que jamones pa que otro los guise y se los coma con frijoles—dijo al ver pasar a la jovencita—. Aquí me quedo con la puela caliente y el plato vació y la cuchara en la mano. Aquí me quedo con el dedo en la boca.

—Chúpeselo hasta que se le seque viejo esqueroso, piojoso, repunoso—dijo la madre enfadadísima.

—Oiga, señora. No hay que verse uno en espejo pa ver si uno es pendejo. Usté es prueba d'eso. Es a su hija a quien admiro de un tiro por su belleza, no a usté cachetona, nalgas aguadas. Además, sepa que tarde o temprano la muchacha que quiere pico, puede ser de un muchacho pobre o de un hombre rico.

—Viejo anducio, sucio. Ojalá que se le trabe la lengua por ser tan marrano—murmuró la madre. En eso vio ella de reojo a Tranquilino que le trababa los dedos.

—Ándale hijita—y la agarró de la mano, doblaron la esquina del callejón y se fueron a casa.

Tranquilino luego se puso a cantar en una voz ronca e imposible de oír el siguiente verso.

Colorín,
colorete.

Venga pacá,
señora y le pico
l'ojete

Apenas acababa él su cancioncilla cuando se acostó boca abajo arriba de un banco para quedarse dormido. A lo lejos se oía música ranchera que venía de Las Chanclas. Más cerca oyó él voces de mujeres. Francisquita y su comadre regresaban de correos cuando Francisquita vio a Tranquilino en el banco.

—Venga, venga. Sígame—le dijo ella a su comadre Sofía. Luego caminaron las dos de puntillas a donde estaba Tranquilino.

—¿Qué va a hacer?—preguntó su comadre.

—Tengo algo sabroso pa Tranquilino que compré cuando paramos en la tienda de don Felipe—contestó Francisquita con un brillo en los ojos.

—Tranqui, Tranqui—dijo al tocarle un hombro.

—¿Qué? ¿Qué? ¿Quién es?—. Reaccionó mientras se restregaba los ojos.

—Tengo algo dulce para ti—y le entregó un piloncillo—. Pruébalo. Te gustará—y Tranquilino tomó dos mordidas bien rápidas. Se notaba que él tenía hambre.

—Ummmm. Está delicioso—expresó él mientras mascaba al quedarse dormido.

—Comadre, ¿qué le dio?

—Es su postre—respondió Francisquita con una sonrisa irónica—. Le darán pujos, o sea, calambres y diarrea pa limpiarle el cuerpo como tamién la boca.

—¡Ay Dios mío, comadre! ¿De dónde saca todo eso?

—¿Qué no sabía usté que más antes yo era una curandera?—comentó con una sonrisita.

—Mientras más vivía yo en Santa Bárbara/Martíneztown, cuanto más sorpresas se me presentaban.

Surprises

THERE WAS NO SCHOOL today so Mom sent me to the little store owned by the elderly don Carlos Buenas. The store was at the end of our street that intersected with Broadway.

"Look, hijito. Here's twenty-five cents. Get a can of chicken-and-rice soup. That's what we're going to have for lunch. It's already eleven o'clock. Are you hungry?"

"Just a little, Mom. I ate two bowls of oatmeal for breakfast."

"Well, get going but don't run."

I took off walking, kicking a tin can that I found on the street through the dirt until I reached the ditch that ran behind don Carlos's store. As I got there I gave the can a swift kick, and it landed in the ditch. The current took it, doing somersaults.

I went inside the store and, as always, found don Carlos behind the meat counter. He was short, wore round gold-plated glasses, and was peering over the counter, chitchatting with a woman.

"Good morning, Junie. I haven't seen you around here in a few days. All okay?"

"Yes, everything's fine."

"What kind of meat do you want today? Ground meat, pork, or baloney?" And he handed me a slice of baloney from the cooler that contained all kinds of fresh meats.

"Today I don't want meat," I responded, as I munched on the baloney that he knew I liked.

"Here," interrupted don Carlos, "take a drink of Delaware Punch.

It's very tasty and healthy. I don't want you to choke on the baloney," and he smiled.

"Thank you very much."

"Okay, Junie, if you don't want meat, what can I do for you?"

"Mom sent me to buy a can of chicken-and-rice soup. Do you have any?"

"Ahhhh. Shiquen soop," said don Carlos in his own brand of English. "It's going to cost you an arm and a leg. No, no, no. It's a joke. Do you have twenty-five cents?"

"I have two bits that Mom gave me," and I handed him the coin.

"Two bits or a quarter, same thing."

As I handed him the money I heard a horrible racket coming from the front of the store. I paid don Carlos and went outside to see what was happening. I couldn't see people but you could hear the commotion coming from behind a truck across the street. I went and saw a man lying face up on the ground. He didn't move; he looked like he was dead. A woman showed up, took out a kerchief from her apron, and fanned his face. All of a sudden the man screamed.

"My legs, my legs!" he shouted, and he tilted his face to one side.

"What happened? What happened?" A desperate voice came from one or two of the women who had shown up to see what was going on.

"He tried to jump onto the truck's running board before I could stop," exclaimed Rufino, the driver, "and he slipped as he opened the door, and I ran over him."

"Who is it, who is it?" asked a woman.

"Oh my God! It's Sisto, my neighbor," shouted the woman who had been at the store with me.

"Sisto works with me," said Rufino. "We must take him immediately to the hospital. Well, don't just stand there," he shouted anxiously. "Help me load him onto the truck."

With the help of two or three women they were able to load the injured man. Rufino took him right away to Saint Joseph's

Hospital in Martíneztown near Longfellow School, about two miles away.

I dashed home with the can of chicken-and-rice soup firmly in one hand, but even so I still dropped it a couple of times. I flew into our little house and put the can on the table.

"Hijito! What took you so long? You had me worried. And look at the can, all bent."

"Mom, you're not going to believe what happened."

"Okay. You can tell me while we eat. Bring in a log of wood to feed the stove to warm up lunch.

"You were hungry, ha! 'The big intestines were about to consume the little ones,' as your dad likes to say."

"Yes, from running so much with the can of chicken-and-rice soup," and I smiled as I downed another spoonful of soup. "Mom, as I started to say, you're not going to believe what happened. No sooner had I paid don Carlos when bang! There was a sound like thunder out in the street. I went out to see and across the street was a man lying on the ground next to this truck. He barely moved—and he hardly spoke. Some women helped the driver load him onto the truck and he took the man to the hospital."

"And do they know who this man is?" Mom inquired.

"I heard the name Sisto, who lives around here."

"Really! Don't tell me it's Sisto Montoya who has a house on the other side of the alley behind us." (These days it's named Martínez Avenue.)

"I don't know, but one of the women who recognized Sisto said that he's her neighbor. It must be the same person—don't you think so, Mom?"

"It surely must be. Sooner or later we'll find out. As the old saying goes, 'If you wish to know who you are, just ask women,'" Mom said, and cracked a smile.

The neighbor who knew Sisto accompanied Rufino to the hospital. She fanned his forehead with her hand, but Sisto didn't react at all. He breathed restlessly. When they got to the hospital,

Rufino went directly to emergency. He knocked on the door and went in.

"I have a very injured man," he said, and immediately two technicians went out with a stretcher on wheels.

They lifted him very carefully and put him onto the stretcher. Then they took him inside the emergency room so a doctor could take a look at him. A nurse walked in with a gown and a pair of slippers for the patient. She went to take off his working boots and suddenly let out a scream that echoed throughout the small room upon seeing the letters SM engraved behind each boot.

"No, no. It can't be," and she pulled the bedsheet back to see the patient's face. "Uncle, uncle, what happened?" exclaimed Jacinta, his niece, who was a nurse at the hospital. Her uncle didn't utter a peep. Quickly a doctor and two assistants tended to him.

A couple of hours later the doctor showed up in the waiting room where Rufino was sitting, and Jacinta joined him. Before the doctor said a word, Rufino stood up.

"Doctor, doctor, how is Sisto? Is he all right or not?"

"Sir, calm down, calm down. Your friend has suffered a badly fractured leg. A specialist will be in charge regarding the best treatment for the injury. Meanwhile, we have given him a tranquilizer to lessen the pain. Do you have any questions?" Rufino shook his head *no*.

Jacinta came in frequently to see how her uncle Sisto was doing. Even with the medicine they gave him, he barely opened his eyes. Around six o'clock that evening he began to grumble and to utter a word here and there that didn't make any sense. Visiting hours came, and Rufino stopped by to see Sisto. He saw his condition and didn't stay long.

That evening Jacinta went home a bit disconsolate, seeing her uncle in that condition. The neighbors already knew of the accident, thanks to the lady who had accompanied Rufino to the hospital after the accident.

The following morning before Jacinta started her shift she went to see how her uncle was doing. She went into the room in her nursing uniform. Her uncle Sisto practically jumped out of bed when he saw her.

"Good heavens! What happened? Where am I?" he burst out loud, almost out of control due to the pain in his legs.

"Calm down, Uncle. You have a broken leg but you're going to be okay."

Little by little, with advice from the doctors and assistance from the nurses, Sisto improved until he was able to leave the hospital. Since he was a widower and without any offspring, Jacinta arranged to take him home.

It took little time before Fortunata, a dear friend of Sisto's who lived in Old Town's Sawmill, found out about the accident. Instead of going to visit him at the hospital, she got in touch with Jacinta and proposed the following.

"Look Jacinta, Sisto's birthday is in two days. What do you say we plan a fiesta that coincides with his return home?"

Jacinta loved the idea and suggested that the celebration be at her house. In that way Sisto wouldn't suspect anything. They proceeded to decorate her house with balloons of all colors and ribbons made from colored crepe paper.

Jacinta, being a nurse, was aware that the number 3 was not only a good number, but was also central to the three stages in life of every human being: birth, marriage, and death. To liven up the atmosphere a bit, Jacinta invited three violinists to welcome her uncle Sisto home. As she entered her house with her uncle in a wheelchair the musicians burst into the popular song, "Allá en el Rancho Grande." All invited guests knew the lyrics and burst into song.

Allá en el rancho grande,
allá donde vivía.
Había una rancherita,
que alegre me decía,
que alegre me decía.

Te voy a hacer unos calzones,
como los que usa el ranchero.
Te los comienzo de lana,
y te los acabo de cuero.
///
Out there on the big ranch,
out there where I used to live.
There was a little ranch gal,
who'd say to me cheerfully,
who'd say to me cheerfully.

I'm going to make you some pants,
like the ones the rancher wears.
I'll start them in wool,
and finish them in leather.

There was endless applause. Sisto was so happy he applauded himself.

After the three violinists finished playing "Allá en el Rancho Grande," a group of boys and girls from the neighborhood came in and broke into song.

Las Mañanitas
Estas son las mañanitas,
que cantaba el Rey David,
hoy por ser día de su santo,
se las cantamos a usted.
Despierte don Sisto, despierte,
mire que ya amaneció.
Ya los pajarillos cantan,
y la luna ya se metió.
///
This is the morning song
that King David sang,

today being your saint's day
we're here to sing the song to you.
Wake up, don Sisto, wake up,
the morning is upon you.
The birds are already singing,
and the moon by now is set.

There was more noisy applause. Sisto, in his wheelchair, was exceedingly happy to see all of his neighbors and friends—above all, the kids. He was known among the children in the barrio because every time a kid had a birthday, Sisto showed up by surprise to play his violin to celebrate along with them.

Fortunata suddenly appeared without Sisto suspecting anything. In an enchanting voice she began serenading him with these words from the popular song, "Las Mañanitas."

¡Qué linda está la mañana
en que vengo a saludarte!
Venimos todos con gusto
y placer a felicitarte.
El día en que tú naciste,
nacieron todas las flores.
Ya viene amaneciendo
ya la luz del día nos dio.
Levántate de mañana,
mira que ya amaneció.
///
How lovely is the morning
that I come to greet you!
We all came full of joy
and pleasure to congratulate you.
The day that you were born
all the flowers were born as well.
The dawn is upon you now,

the sun is shining brightly.
Arise early,
dawn is upon you.

As Fortunata finished singing she approached Sisto, gave him a warm embrace, and kissed him on the forehead. He was speechless. The silence didn't last long. All of a sudden Rufino walked in with a basketful of bizcochitos that sparkled with cinnamon.

"Happy birthday to you! Happy birthday, dear Sisto!" he shouted, and he handed him the bizcochitos, which Jacinta and Fortunata shared with the guests.

Sisto had never had such a joyful birthday. It was an unforgettable fiesta, in particular the kids and Fortunata who had sung and the violinists who had accompanied them.

Sooner or later Sisto forgot about the accident and returned to work with Rufino at the Albuquerque Iron and Foundry Company.

A surprise and a happy ending, but there would be other surprises to come when I drew water from Grandma Lale's pump.

Sorpresas

HOY NO HUBO ESCUELA de manera que mamá me mandó a la tienda del viejito don Carlos Buenas la cual estaba a fines de la calle nuestra que pega con Broadway.

—Mira, hijito. Aquí tienes dos reales. Te compras un bote de arroz con pollo. Es lo que vamos a lonchar. Ya son las once. ¿Tienes hambre?

—Un poquito nada más amá. Me comí dos ollas de aveno pal almuerzo.

—Pues anda vete pero no vayas corriendo.

Me fui andando, dándole patadas en la tierra a un jarro que hallé en la calle hasta que llegué a la acequia que corría detrás de la tiendita de don Carlos. Al llegar le di una patada fuerte al jarro y fue a dar en la acequia. La corriente se lo llevó dándose marometas.

Entré en la tienda y como siempre hallé a don Carlos detrás del mostrador de carnes. Él era bajito, usaba anteojos redondos dorados, y estaba mirando por encima del mostrador platicando con una señora.

—Buenos días, Junie. Hace días que no te encuentras por aquí. ¿Todo bien?

—Sí, todo bien.

—¿Qué clase de carne quieres hoy? ¿Molida, de marrano, o chorizo?—y me dio una rebanada de chorizo de la hielera que contenía toda clase de carnes frescas.

—Hoy no quiero carne—le respondí mientras me mascaba el chorizo el cual él sabía que me gustaba.

—Toma—interrumpió don Carlos—. Bébete un trago de *Delaware Punch*. Es muy sabrosa y saludable. No quiero que te vayas a ahogar con el chorizo—y se sonrió.

—Muchas gracias.

—Bueno, Junie, si no quieres carne, ¿qué se te ofrece?

—Mi amá me mandó a que comprara un bote de arroz con pollo. ¿Tiene o no?

—Ahhhh. *Shiquen soop*—dijo don Carlos en un inglés mocho—. Te va costar una pata y la mitá de la otra. No, no, no. Es un chiste. ¿Tienes veinte y cinco centavos?

—Tengo dos reales que me dio mi amá—y le entregué la moneda.

—Dos reales o veinte y cinco centavos. Es lo mismo.

Al entregarle el dinero oí un ruidazo delante de la tienda. Le pagué a don Carlos y salí a ver qué pasaba. No veía a gente pero se oía el alboroto que venía de detrás de una troca al otro lado de la calle. Fui y vi a un hombre boca arriba en la tierra. No se movía; parecía que estaba muerto. Llegó una mujer, sacó un pañuelo de su delantal, y le abanicó la cara. De pronto gritó el hombre.

—¡Mis piernas, mis piernas!—e hizo la cara a un lado.

—¿Qué pasó? ¿Qué pasó?— Se oyó una voz desesperada que venía de una de las dos o tres mujeres que se presentaron para ver qué pasaba.

—Quiso brincar él en el estribo de la troca antes que yo parara—exclamó Rufino, el chofer—y se resbaló al abrir la puerta y lo trampé.

—¿Quién es, quién es?—preguntó una señora.

—¡Ay Dios mío! Es Sisto, vecino mío—gritó la señora que estaba en la tienda conmigo.

—Sisto trabaja conmigo—dijo Rufino—. Hay que llevarlo pronto al hospital. Pues no se queden ahi paradas—vociferó ansiosamente—. Ayúdenme a echarlo en la troca.

Con la ayuda de dos o tres mujeres pudieron cargar al herido en la troca. Rufino lo llevó de prisa al Hospital de San José en Martíneztown cerca de la Escuela de Longfellow a unas dos millas de lejos.

Yo me fui a casa corriendo con el bote de arroz con pollo firme en una mano pero aun así se me cayó un par de veces. Entré volando en nuestra casita y puse el bote sobre la mesa.

—¡Hijito! ¿Por qué te tardaste tanto? Aquí me tenías con la pena. Y mira el bote como viene too atachao.

—Amá, no vas a creer lo que pasó.

—Güeno. Ya me dirás mientras comemos. Tráete un leño pa la estufa pa calentar el lonche.

—Tenías hambre, ¿eh? "Ya se comían las grandes a las chiquitas"—como le gusta decir a tu papá.

—Sí, de tanto correr con el bote de arroz con pollo—y me sonreí al echarme otra cucharada de sopa en la boca—. Amá, como te decía. No vas a creer lo que pasó. Nomás en cuanto le pagué a don Carlos y ¡zas! Hubo como un trueno en la calle. Salí a ver y allí al otro lado de la calle estaba un hombre en la tierra junto a esta troca. Apenas se movía, y casi ni hablaba. Unas mujeres le ayudaron al chofer a echarlo en la troca y él se lo llevó al hospital.

—¿Y se sabe quién es este hombre?—preguntó mamá.

—Oí el nombre Sisto que vive por acá.

—¡A poco! No me digas que es Sisto Montoya el que tiene casa al otro lado del callejón detrás de nosotros. (Estos días es Martínez Avenue.)

—No sé pero una de las mujeres que reconoció a Sisto dijo que es su vecino. Debe ser la mesma persona, ¿no crees amá?

—Seguro que sí. Tarde o temprano sabremos. Como luego dice el dicho, dijo mamá, "Si quieres saber quién eres, pregúntaselo a mujeres." Y soltó una risita mamá.

La señora vecina que conocía a Sisto acompañó a Rufino al hospital. Ella le abanicaba la frente con la mano, pero Sisto no reaccionaba del todo. Respiraba de una manera inquieta. Cuando llegaron al hospital Rufino se fue directamente a emergencia. Tocó la puerta y entró.

—Traigo un hombre muy lastimado—dijo él, y en seguida salieron dos técnicos con una camilla en ruedas.

Lo levantaron con mucho cuidado y lo pusieron en la camilla. Luego lo metieron en la sala de emergencia para que lo viera un médico. Entró una enfermera con un camisón y un par de chinelas para el paciente. Fue a quitarle las botas de trabajo y de pronto pegó un grito que retumbó por la pequeña sala al ver las letras SM inscritas detrás de cada bota.

—No, no. No puede ser—dijo ella, y jaló la sábana para ver la cara del paciente—. Tío, tío, ¿qué pasó?—exclamó con gran sorpresa Jacinta, su nieta que era enfermera en el hospital. Su tío no dijo ni pío. En seguida lo atendieron un médico y los dos asistentes.

Un par de horas más tarde se presentó el médico en la sala de espera (Jacinta lo acompañó) donde Rufino estaba esperando. Antes de que dijera una palabra el médico, Rufino se puso de pie.

—Doctor, doctor, ¿cómo sigue Sisto? ¿Está bien o no?

—Con calma, señor, con calma. Su amigo ha sufrido una mala fractura de una pierna. Un especialista se encargará tocante al mejor tratamiento para la herida. Entretanto, le hemos dado un calmante para aliviar el dolor. Hoy por la tarde tal vez permitan visitas. Habría que consultar con las enfermeras. ¿Tiene preguntas?—. Rufino señaló que no.

Jacinta entraba con frecuencia a ver cómo seguía su tío Sisto. Hasta con la medicina que le dieron apenas abría los ojos. A eso de las seis por la tarde empezó a refunfuñar y a decir una que otra palabra pero no tenían mucho sentido. Llegaron las horas de visita, y pasó Rufino a ver a Sisto. Vio cómo seguía y no se quedó largo tiempo.

Esa tarde se fue Jacinta a casa un poco desconsolada de ver a su tío en aquel estado. Ya los vecinos sabían del accidente, gracias a la mujer que acompañó a Rufino al hospital después del accidente.

A la mañana siguiente antes de empezar su turno Jacinta fue a ver cómo había amanecido su tío. Entró en la habitación en su traje de enfermera. Su tío Sisto por poco salta de la cama al verla.

—¡Madre mía! ¿Qué pasó? ¿Dónde estoy?—. Prorrumpió casi fuera de sí quejándose del dolor de las piernas.

—Tranquilo, tío. Usté tiene una pierna rota pero va a sanar.

Poco a poco con consejos de los médicos y la asistencia de las enfermeras fue mejorando Sisto hasta que pudo dejar el hospital. Como era viudo y sin hijos Jacinta hizo arreglos para llevarlo a casa.

Tardó poco en enterarse del accidente Fortunata, amiga íntima de Sisto que vivía en Sawmill de la Plaza Vieja. En vez de ir a visitarlo en el hospital se puso en contacto con Jacinta y le propuso lo siguiente.

—Mira Jacinta, el cumpleaños de Sisto es dentro de dos días. ¿Qué te parece si planeamos una fiesta que coincida con su regreso a casa?

A Jacinta le encantó la idea y sugirió que la celebración fuera en su casa. Así Sisto no sospecharía nada. Procedieron a decorar la casa de Jacinta con globos de todos colores y listones de papel crepé de distintos colores.

Siendo que Jacinta era enfermera ella estaba al tanto que el número 3 no solamente es un buen número sino que conforma fundamental con las tres etapas de la vida de todo ser humano: nacimiento, matrimonio, y fallecimiento. Para animar el ambiente un poco, Jacinta invitó a tres violinistas a que tocaran para darle la bienvenida a su tío Sisto. Al entrar ella en su casa con su tío en la silla de ruedas rompieron los músicos con la canción popular "Allá en el Rancho Grande." Todos los invitados sabían la letra y se pusieron a cantar.

Allá en el rancho grande,
allá donde vivía.
Había una rancherita,
que alegre me decía,
que alegre me decía.

Te voy a hacer unos calzones,

como los que usa el ranchero.
Te los comienzo de lana,
y te los acabo de cuero.

Hubo un sinfín de aplausos. Sisto mismo dio sus palmadas de lo contento que estaba.

Al terminar de tocar los tres violinistas "Allá en el rancho grande," entró un grupo de niños y niñas de la vecindad y rompieron en canto.

Las Mañanitas
Estas son las mañanitas,
que cantaba el Rey David,
hoy por ser día de su santo,
se las cantamos a usted.
Despierte don Sisto, despierte,
mire que ya amaneció.
Ya los pajarillos cantan,
y la luna ya se metió.

Hubo más aplausos ruidosos. Sisto en su silla de ruedas seguía rete contento al ver a todos sus vecinos y amigos, sobre todo a los niños. Él tenía fama entre los niños del barrio porque cada vez que un niño tenía cumpleaños, Sisto aparecía de sorpresa y tocaba su violín para festejar junto con ellos.

Fortunata se presentó repentinamente sin que Sisto sospechara nada. En una encantadora voz se puso a serenarlo con estas palabras de la canción popular "Las Mañanitas."

¡Qué linda está la mañana
en que vengo a saludarte!
Venimos todos con gusto
y placer a felicitarte.
El día en que tú naciste,

nacieron todas las flores.
Ya viene amaneciendo
ya la luz del día nos dio.
Levántate de mañana,
mira que ya amaneció.

Al acabar de cantar Fortunata se acercó a Sisto, le dio un cariñoso abrazo, y le plantó un beso en la frente. Él se quedó sin palabras. No tardó en romperse el silencio. De buenas a primeras entró Rufino con un cesto lleno de bizcochitos que brillaban con canela.

—¡Felicidades en tu día! ¡Felicidades en tu día querido Sisto!— expresó Rufino en voz alta, y le entregó los bizcochitos los cuales Jacinta y Fortunata repartieron entre los huéspedes.

Jamás había tenido Sisto un cumpleaños tan alegre. Fue una fiesta inolvidable, en particular los niños y Fortunata que le cantaron, y los violinistas que los acompañaron.

Tarde o temprano se olvidó Sisto del accidente y regresó a trabajar con Rufino en el *Albuquerque Iron and Foundry Company*.

Un final sorprendente y feliz, pero ya habría otras sorpresas que parecían ocurrir mientras yo sacaba agua de la pompa de mi abuelita Lale.

left to right: Rita Ruelas, Nasario's cousin; Julianita, Nasario's sister; and Agapita López-García, Nasario's mother, with daughter Elsie in her arms. Grandma's shed, Santa Barbara / Martíneztown, 1945. Photograph from Nasario García's private collection.

Teodorita García-Ruelas washing and drying mattress wool, with daughter Rita. Santa Barbara / Martíneztown, circa 1945. Photograph from Nasario García's private collection.

Santa Barbara, historic school, National Register of Historic Place and State Register of Cultural Properties, 2024. Photograph courtesy of Nasario García.

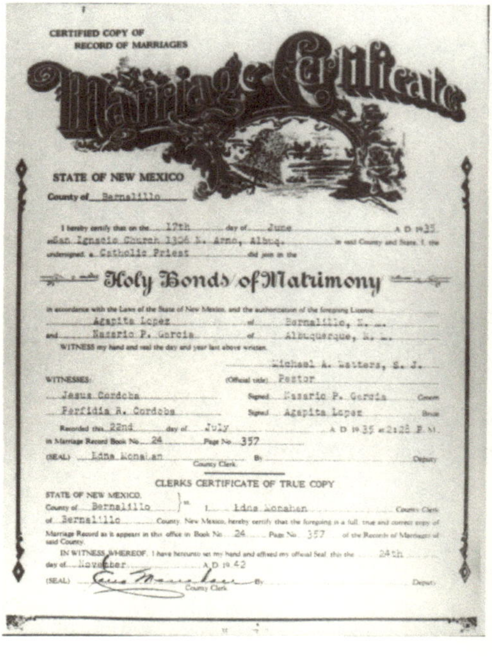

CERTIFIED COPY OF
RECORD OF MARRIAGES

Marriage Certificate

STATE OF NEW MEXICO
County of Bernalillo

I hereby certify that on the 17th day of June A.D. 1935 at San Ignacio Church 1306 N. Arno, Albuq. in said County and State, I, the undersigned, a Catholic Priest did join in the

Holy Bonds of Matrimony

in accordance with the Laws of the State of New Mexico, and the authorization of the foregoing License
Agapita Lopez of Bernalillo, N. M.
and Nasario P. Garcia of Albuquerque, N. M.
WITNESS my hand and seal the day and year last above written.

Michael A. Watters, S. J.
(Official title) Pastor

WITNESSES:
Jesus Cordoba
Perfidia R. Cordoba

Signed Nasario P. Garcia Groom
Signed Agapita Lopez Bride

Recorded this 22nd day of July A.D. 1935 at 2:25 P.M.
in Marriage Record Book No. 24 Page No. 357
(SEAL) Edna Monahan County Clerk By Deputy

CLERKS CERTIFICATE OF TRUE COPY

STATE OF NEW MEXICO,
County of Bernalillo } ss. I, Edna Monahan County Clerk of Bernalillo County, New Mexico, hereby certify that the foregoing is a full, true and correct copy of Marriage Record as it appears in this office in Book No. 24 Page No. 357 of the Records of Marriages of said County.

IN WITNESS WHEREOF, I have hereunto set my hand and affixed my official Seal, this the 24th day of November A.D. 1942

(SEAL) County Clerk By Deputy

Nasario P. García and Agapita López. Marriage certificate, San Ignacio Church, Santa Barbara / Martíneztown, 1935. Photograph from Nasario García's private collection.

Nasario P. García and Agapita López, wedding, San Ignacio Church, Martíneztown, 1935. Photograph from Nasario García's private collection.

Jesús Córdova and Perfilia Córdova, wedding godparents (*padrinos*), standing; Nasario P. García and Agapita López, seated, Bernalillo, New Mexico, 1935. Photograph from Nasario García's private collection.

left to right: Emilia and Eulogio Lucero, wife and husband; Eulogio Jr., groom; Eremita Griego, bride; Trinidad Griego, grandmother, and Higinio Griego, son; and Emilia and Teodoro García, bride's paternal grandparents. Eremita Griego and Eulogio Lucero Jr.'s wedding, Santa Barbara / Martíneztown, circa 1946. Photograph courtesy of Nasario García.

top: Teodoro García, Emilia García, and Sara Sánchez, Santa Barbara / Martíneztown, 1958; *bottom*: Luis Sánchez, Teodoro García, and Emilia García. Photograph courtesy of Julia García-Gurulé.

left to right: Vincent Gurulé, Alfredo Sánchez, Luis Sánchez, Donaldo Orozco (?), and Benny Montoya (?), El Porvenir Bar, Santa Barbara / Martíneztown, undated. Photograph courtesy of Julia García-Gurulé.

Julia García and Ed Gurulé, wedding, Santa Bárbara / Martíneztown, 1958. Photograph courtesy of Julia García-Gurulé.

Antonio P. García and Taida Sánchez-García, daughter Julia García's wedding, 1958. Photograph courtesy of Julia García-Gurulé.

John, Johnny, and Big John

BEFORE EATING SUPPER, I went to draw water for Mom from Grandma Lale's pump in front of her house. I put the empty bucket on the ground to collect the water. I liked the up-and-down movement of pumping water. How the water came from underneath the ground and reached the top and into the bucket fascinated me, but was something that I hardly comprehended. On the other hand, I had been raised with magical things at the ranch, which were accepted though not always explained.

The bucket was almost full when suddenly I heard some footsteps behind me. I turned around, thinking it was my grandma who was about to tickle me, even though she hardly ever joked around. But no; it was a stranger.

"Good afternoon, young man," he uttered in an authoritarian manner as though I wasn't a kid of nine years old. "I'm don Claudio. I'm thirsty. Will you give me a drink of water?"

"Yes sir, but I don't have a cup or a glass."

"A cup, whether with or without a handle, only at home," exclaimed the stranger in a quasi-poetic way. "That's what these hands are for," and he put them under the pump to toss water into his mouth. "Okay. Pump!" And I pumped really hard, splashing his entire face. "Not so fast. Slowly," he said, and he wiped his face with his shirt sleeves.

Don Claudio took his sips, and with the back of his hand wiped the water dripping like saliva down both sides of his mouth.

"By the way, what is your name?" This time he was more informal.

"Junie García. I'm the grandson of Grandma Emilia, who lives here. It's her pump."

"And what kind of a name is Junie? Like Juan?"

"No, the name comes from Junior. Junie is my nickname."

"Aha! I ask because in this neighborhood we already have three Juans: Juan, Juanito, y Juanote. We don't need another Juan," he pointed out in a sarcastic way, even though I didn't quite understand his string of Juans.

"And why do they have such similar names?" I asked.

"Because all three are cut from the same cloth. Do you understand me?"

"I don't think so."

"Because all three are homos, *jotos*," he burst out impatiently. "Do you understand now what I'm telling you or not?"

"I believe so," I answered, because I knew well what the word joto meant.

"Okay, thank you very much for the water," and he bid me goodbye.

As he took off, I noticed that he had an odd walk. With each step that he took, his right leg flew up in the air and with both hands he immediately pulled it back toward him so as not to lose his balance and fall. I felt really sorry for him. At that moment my grandma appeared on the porch.

"Who were you talking to, hijito?"

"To a man named don Claudio."

"Ah, don Claudio. He's known as the one with the loose leg in the air. He's famous. And do you know why? Because he gives nicknames to a lot of people in the barrio. And do you know something else that's very strange? Very few people know that the name Claudio means lame. Now that's really weird. I'm sure my God Almighty meant good intentions for him to be baptized with that name."

"Okay, Grandma. I'm off. Mom's waiting for the water," and I took off in a hurry. I couldn't help but spill some of it, given that the bucket was full.

"Ah, hijito. What were you doing? Did the water have a hard time coming up from the ground?" she asked jokingly.

"Mom, I bet there's one thing you don't know. This man with a loose leg came to ask me for a drink of water. His leg flies in the air when he walks."

"Ah, it must be don Claudio. There's no one else that I know of in the neighborhood who has a loose leg. People say that he also has a loose tongue. He nicknames lots of residents."

"Like what, Mom?"

"I don't know. Perhaps your dad knows. But if you really want to know, go ask your grandma. She's lived here many years. She knows, for sure."

"Okay. After eating supper I'll go talk to her."

We ate supper and I helped Mom wash and dry the dishes before I went to see Grandma. I knocked on the kitchen screen door.

"Who is it?" (*¿Quién es?*)

"Old man Inés," I responded, in a humorous sort of a way.

"Who else is there?" (*¿Quién es el otro?*) she responded jokingly, even though my grandma was a very serious person.

"The tattered old man" (*El viejo roto*), I answered, and went into the kitchen. I found Grandma seated near the stove with her back toward the window.

"I thought you were don Claudio, the one with the loose leg," and she laughed.

"That's why I came. You told me that he names people in the barrio but you didn't tell me why."

"Listen, hijito. Many years ago, don Claudio was a grave digger here at the Santa Barbara Cemetery. One day he and two or three companions went to dig a grave for a neighbor who had died. It had rained the night before, therefore the soil was damp, and it was not hard to stick the shovel in the ground to dig the grave. They were about to finish when don Claudio had the misfortune of slipping.

He did a somersault and landed in the grave. His pals burst out laughing but they quickly realized that don Claudio wasn't moving. Then my son Antonio lowered his shovel and asked him to hold onto the handle to pull him out. 'No, no. I can't. My leg, my leg! There's something wrong with it. Or it's the hip bone. I can't move.'"

My grandma continued.

"Then your uncle Ramón, the most muscular of the group, jumped into the grave and with his hands on don Claudio's butt, pushed him upward, and they got him out but he couldn't walk. Okay, the story has it that the doctors couldn't do anything because don Claudio complained of the excruciating pain. Eventually he was able to walk, but his right leg was loose and out of control. Every time he took a step his leg flew into the air. Sooner or later the people started saying 'there comes don Claudio, the one with the loose leg.' They laughed at the strange manner in which he walked—and continues to walk. That's why he started giving nicknames to people who made fun of him."

"Poor don Claudio."

"Yes and no, hijito. Years ago he was a good man but one day he lost a screw. Nowadays he has his ugly moods, just like many other people, but I get along with him just fine. Ah, I almost forgot."

"What, Grandma?"

"Tomorrow is Saint John's Day. You know what it is, don't you?"

"Yes, Grandma. We used to celebrate it at the ranch in Ojo del Padre with horse races."

"Very well; here there won't be any races, but elderly couples in particular stroll down our street in the late afternoon after a short siesta. They chitchat and have a good time. You'll see."

"And don Claudio also?"

"No doubt, although he is a widower and doesn't have a female companion. But there are others like don Claudio who go strolling alone or with friends. They do it to find out what's going on. They like to gossip."

Next day, no sooner said than done, I stood in front of my grandma's house, which faced the street. It wasn't long before she joined me.

"Have the people started their strolls?"

"A few," I responded.

"Just wait a bit. More will come. To go walking after eating is also good for digesting your food."

"Look, Grandma! There comes don Claudio with two men."

"Good afternoon, neighbor. How are you?"

"I'm well, thanks be to God," responded my grandma.

"And who is this young man?" There was a pause. "Good heavens! I almost forgot. He gave me water from your pump the other day. Okay, we're going to continue walking," don Claudio said, and he and his pals departed.

"Hijito, you want to go with me for a stroll? You can be my partner."

"Why of course, Grandma. I'll go tell Mom and Dad I'm going with you for a walk."

"Go! I'll wait for you here on the porch." I ran and returned immediately.

My grandma and I took off. We headed toward the Santa Barbara Cemetery till we reached the end of the street and then turned around. At that given moment I recognized don Claudio's voice. He and his pals were chatting on the front porch about three houses from my grandma's house. Just about then I saw three young guys, of different sizes and heights, coming toward us. They were about seventeen or eighteen years old. But what caught my attention more than anything else was the fact that they were holding hands. I didn't say anything to Grandma. I remained quiet.

I heard don Claudio's voice once again, and laughter coming from his buddies.

"Here, here! Welcome Juan, Juanito, y Juanote. Today is Saint John's Day so that you can celebrate your day snuggled together," shouted don Claudio. More laughter ensued, but then horselaughs erupted.

"Grandma, why are those men laughing? And why do the three boys practically have the same name?"

"Ah, they're names that don Claudio gave to them. As I told you once, he's famous for naming people in the community in an ugly and unpleasant manner."

"But Grandma, why are those men laughing and laughing?"

"Because the cantankerous don Claudio, with a loose tongue, thinks that those young boys are homos. As mischievous as they are, they walk hand-in-hand just to mock him."

I got tongue-tied and didn't know what to say. Perhaps there was nothing left to say. Grandma had said it all.

Juan, Juanito, y Juanote

ANTES DE CENAR FUI a sacar agua para mamá en la pompa de Abuelita Lale delante de su casa. Puse la cubeta vacía sobre la tierra para recoger el agua. A mí me gustaba el movimiento de pompear agua para arriba y para abajo. Cómo subía el agua desde debajo de la tierra hacia arriba y luego llegaba a la cubeta me fascinaba, pero era algo que yo apenas entendía. Por otra parte, yo me había criado con lo mágico en el rancho, lo cual se aceptaba aunque no siempre se explicara.

Me faltaba poco para llenar la cubeta cuando de pronto sentí unos pasos detrás de mí. Volteé a ver creyendo que era mi abuelita que estaba por hacerme cosquillas aunque ella casi nunca chisteaba. Pero no, era un desconocido.

—Buenas tardes joven—, me saludó en forma autoritaria como si yo no fuera un niño de nueve años—. Yo soy don Claudio. Traigo sé. ¿Me das un trago de agua?

—Sí señor, pero no tengo taza o vaso.

—Ya sea taza con asa o sin asa sólo en casa—exclamó el extranjero de una manera poética—. Para eso son estas manos—y las puso bajo la pompa para echarse agua en la boca—. Bueno. ¡Pompéale!—y pompeé bien recio, salpicándole toda la cara—. No tan fuerte. Despacito—, y se limpió la cara con las mangas de la camisa.

Tomó don Claudio sus sorbos y con la parte detrás de la mano se secó los chorros de agua que le colgaban como babas por ambos lados de la boca.

—A propósito, ¿cómo te llamas tú?—esta vez de una manera más informal.

—Junie García. Yo soy el nieto de mi agüelita Emilia que vive aquí. La pompa es de ella.

—¿Y qué clase de nombre es Junie? ¿Cómo Juan?

—No, el nombre viene de Junior. Junie es mi sobrenombre.

—¡Aja! Te pregunto porque en este barrio ya tenemos tres Juanes: Juan, Juanito, y Juanote. No necesitamos otro Juan—indicó de una manera sarcástica aunque yo no entendí su chorro de Juanes.

—¿Y por qué ellos tienen esos nombres tan parecidos?—le pregunté.

—Porque los tres están cortados con la misma tijera. ¿Me entiendes?

—Creo que no.

—Porque los tres son jotitos, pirujos—prorrumpió de una manera impaciente—. ¿Ahora entiendes lo que te digo o no?

—Creo que sí—le respondí porque entendía bien yo lo que quería decir la palabra joto.

—Bueno, muchas gracias por l'agua—y se despidió.

Al marcharse me di cuenta que andaba de una manera rara. Con cada paso que daba se le soltaba la pierna derecha en el aire y con ayuda de las dos manos pronto la recogía hacia él para no perder su balance y caerse. Mi dio mucha lástima. En eso salió mi abuelita por el portal.

—¿Con quién hablabas hijito?

—Con un hombre que se llama don Claudio.

—Ah, don Claudio. Se conoce como el de la pierna suelta en el aire. Él tiene fama. ¿Y sabes por qué? Porque les pone sobrenombres a muchos en el barrio. ¿Y sabes otra cosa muy extraña? Poca gente sabe que el nombre Claudio quiere decir cojo. Eso sí que es extraño. Seguro que mi Tatita Dios quiso que le pusieran ese nombre con buenas intenciones.

—Güeno agüelita. Ya me voy. Mamá está esperando l'agua—y

me fui de prisa. No pude menos de salpicar parte siendo que la cubeta estaba llena.

—Ah, hijito. ¿Qué hacías? ¿Qué no salía l'agua de la tierra?—preguntó bromeando.

—Amá, a qué no sabes algo. Vino este hombre con una pierna suelta a pedirme agua que beber. Se le vuela la pierna en el aire cuando anda.

—Ah, debe ser don Claudio. No hay otro en la vecindá que yo sepa que tenga una pierna suelta. Se dice tamién que tiene una lengua suelta. Les pone sobrenombres a muchos residentes.

—¿Cómo qué amá?

—No sé. Tal vez tu papá sepa. Pero si de veras quieres saber, ve pregúntale a tu agüelita. Ella lleva munchos años aquí. Por cierto sabe.

—Güeno. Después de cenar voy y hablo con ella.

Cenamos y le ayudé a mamá a lavar y secar los trastes antes de ir a ver a mi abuelita. Toqué la puerta de alambre de la cocina.

—¿Quién es?

—El viejo Inés—le contesté de una manera chistosa.

—¿Quién es el otro?—respondió ella a pesar de que mi abuelita era una persona muy seria.

—El viejo roto—contesté y entré en la cocina. La encontré sentada cerca de la estufa con la espalda a la ventana.

—Creí que eras don Claudio el de la pierna suelta—y soltó ella la risa.

—Es por eso que vine. Usté me dijo que él le pone nombres a la gente del barrio pero no me dijo por qué.

—Mira hijito. Hace munchos años don Claudio era un saca-sepulcros aquí en el cementerio de Santa Bárbara. Un día fueron él y dos o tres compañeros a sacar un sepulcro para un vecino que había muerto. Llovió la noche anterior de manera que la tierra estaba mojada y no costó trabajo clavar la pala para hacer el hoyo. Ya estaban para terminar cuando tuvo la mala suerte don Claudio que se resbaló. Se dio una marometa y fue a dar en el sepulcro. Sus compañeros soltaron la risa pero pronto se dieron cuenta que don Claudio no se movía. Luego mi hijo Antonio bajó su pala y le dijo que se prendiera del cabo para sacarlo. "No, no. No puedo. ¡La pierna, la pierna! Algo le pasa. O es el cuadril. No puedo moverme."

Continuó mi abuelita.

—Entonces tu tío Ramón el más garrudo del grupo brincó en el sepulcro y con las manos en las nalgas de don Claudio lo empujó parriba y lo sacaron, pero no podía andar. Güeno, el cuento es que los doctores no pudieron hacer nada porque don Claudio se quejaba del dolor insoportable. Por fin pudo andar, pero la pierna derecha le quedó como suelta y fuera de control. Cada vez que daba un paso la pierna se le volaba en el aire. Tarde o temprano la gente empezó con que "ahi viene don Claudio, el de la pierna suelta." Se burlaban de la manera extraña que él andaba—y sigue andando—. Por eso él comenzó a ponerle nombres a gente que se burlaba de él.

—Pobrecito don Claudio.

—Sí y no hijito. Años atrás él era un buen hombre pero un día se le voltearon las muelas al revés. Hoy día tiene sus malas greñas como mucha otra gente, pero yo me llevo bien con él. Ah, por poco se me olvida.

—¿Qué agüelita?

—Mañana es el Día de San Juan. Ya sabes lo que es, ¿no?

—Sí agüelita. Lo celebrábamos en el rancho en Ojo del Padre con corridas de caballo.

—Güeno, aquí no habrá corridas, pero los matrimonios mayores en particular se pasean por nuestra calle en la tarde después de tomar una siestecita. Platican y pasan un buen rato. Ya verás.

—¿Y tamién don Claudio?

—Seguro que sí aunque él es viudo y no tiene compañera. Pero hay otros como don Claudio que salen de paseo solos o con amigos. Lo hacen para ver quién va y quién viene. Les gusta mitotear.

Al día siguiente dicho y hecho. Me puse al frente de la casa de mi abuelita que daba a la calle. No tardó en acompañarme ella.

—¿Ya empezó la gente sus paseos?

—Unas cuantas—le respondí.

—Espérate un poquito. Ya vendrán más. Salir andando después de comer tamién es bueno pa que se te baje la comida.

—¡Mire agüelita! Ahi viene don Claudio con dos hombres.

—Buenas tardes, vecina. ¿Cómo le va?

—Pues estoy bien, gracias a Dios—le respondió mi abuelita.

—¿Y quién es este joven?—hubo una pausa—. ¡Ay caramba! Por poco se me olvida. Él me dio agua de su pompa el otro día. Bueno, vamos seguir andando—dijo don Claudio, y se marcharon él y sus compañeros.

—Hijito, ¿quieres ir de paseo conmigo?—me preguntó mi abuelita—. Puedes ser mi compañero.

—Como que no agüelita. Pero voy a decirles a en papá y a mi amá que voy de paseo con usté.

—¡Ve! Aquí te espero en el portal. Fui corriendo y volví en seguida.

Salimos yo y mi abuelita. Pescamos al rumbo del cementerio de Santa Bárbara hasta llegar a fines de la calle y luego dimos la vuelta. En ese dado momento reconocí la voz de don Claudio. Él y sus compañeros estaban platicando en el portal a unas tres casas de la casa de mi abuelita. En eso vi a tres jóvenes de diferentes tamaños y alturas que venían caminando hacia nosotros. Tenían sus diez y siete o diez y ocho años. Pero lo que me llamó la atención más que nada fue que venían tomados de la mano. Yo no le dije nada a mi abuelita. Me quedé calladito.

Volví a oír la voz de don Claudio y unas risas de sus cuates.

—¡Epa, epa! Bien venidos Juan, Juanito, y Juanote. Hoy es el Día de San Juan para que ustedes celebren su día apretados juntitos—chilló don Claudio. Hubo más risas, pero luego se convirtieron en risotadas.

Agüelita, ¿por qué están riéndose esos hombres? ¿Y por qué los tres muchachos casi tiene el mesmo nombre?

—Ah, son nombres que les ha puesto don Claudio. Como te dije una vez, él tiene fama de bautizar a gente en del barrio de una manera desagradable y grotesca.

—Pero agüelita, ¿por qué estaban esos hombres risa y risa?

—Porque el mala cacha y lengua suelta de don Claudio cree que esos jóvenes son jotitos. Ellos por traviesos que son caminan de la mano simplemente pa burlarse de él.

Se me atoraron las palabras y no supe qué decir. Quizás no quedaba más que decir. Mi abuelita lo había dicho todo.

The Machete Brothers

NOT AS LIGHTHEARTED AS the three Juans in the previous story, but entertaining nonetheless, are the machete brothers. I remember the day quite clearly. It was a Saturday. I had just finished eating lunch and I went outside to enjoy my lollipop in the shade. I sat very comfortably on the ground with my back up against the wall of our tiny adobe home. I stretched my legs. The round orange candy I had bought the day before at don Carlos Buenas's store it could scarcely fit into my mouth. Little by little it got smaller with every lick.

My joy, all of a sudden, was interrupted by a loud racket. I couldn't tell where it was coming from. I cupped an ear. I heard voices. I stood up and saw, across the back alley (nowadays it's Martínez Avenue), two men shouting in the front yard of this house. They were cursing, insulting, and threatening each other. At an unexpected moment I saw them waving their arms in the air and sparks flying from two huge knives. I got scared and ran to tell Mom what I had just seen.

"*Amá, amá*. There's two men arguing and cursing at each other."

"Let's go see. It doesn't cost anything. I'll follow you," she said, and we headed over to look through the wooden fence that faced the alley. "Good heavens! Those idiots are going to kill each other. Just look at the sparks flying from those machetes. I believe they're drunk."

"Mom, what are machetes?"

"Oh, hijito. I don't know how to explain it. Go ask your father. He knows more about those things. He's over at your grandma's house."

I went, knocked on the kitchen door, and went in. They were drinking coffee and discussing who knows what.

"Good afternoon, hijito. What winds bring you around here?"

"I came to ask Dad something."

"And why not me?" she said, smiling.

"*Apá*, what's a machete?"

"Ah, don't tell me," interrupted my grandma before Dad could respond. "I bet the machete brothers are at it with their machetes."

"But what are machetes?" I asked once again.

"Every Saturday afternoon," continued my grandma, "they get drunk and come out to their patio and sparks fly from those long, sharp machetes. They resemble the knife that your grandpa uses at the ranch when he butchers a hog. It's scary to see those brothers with their machetes."

"Grandma, don't they hurt or cut each other?"

"Nah. No harm at all. That's the way drunkards are. They're luckier than the devil."

"But don't these brothers have real names?"

"They're the Vallejos. One is named Carpio and the other is Plácido. They work for a company called Pura Harina (Purina). That's where they sell food for dogs and cats."

"Is that why they fight like cats and dogs, Grandma?"

"That's not funny," interjected my father.

"In any case," continued my grandma, "the money they earn at Pura Harina is how they buy their beer."

"But Mom," added my father, "they're married, aren't they?"

"Yes, the two of them live with their wives in that same house that's large like mine."

"But as far as I can tell, you never see their wives," Dad commented.

"Ah, my dear son, don't kid yourself. Every once in a while they get drunk right along with their husbands. They come out practically naked, pulling at each other's hair, and spewing absurdities. You won't believe what comes out of their mouths."

"Okay, Grandma, I gotta go. I'm going to tell Mom what a machete is."

Well sure enough, just about every Saturday afternoon, you could hear the whacks from the machetes, a swear word here and there, and the wives' nonsense. All of that echoed throughout the alley.

There was an honorary deputy in Santa Barbara whose name was Justín Naranjos. He and his little truck were well-known. The neighbors went to him with complaints regarding the machete brothers although some people saw them more as something amusing and non-threatening.

Another Saturday was upon us and Deputy Naranjos, a big, strong man, tried to calm the machete brothers, but it was to no avail. Tired of the rumpus and complaints against Plácido and Carpio, he loaded each one into the bed of his small truck and took them to the Santa Barbara Cemetery where the deputy was a grave-digger. He locked them up in a little room so they could spend the night and get over their drunkenness. In the morning he gave each one a cup of black coffee before he let them go home. They had barely finished their coffee when Carpio stood up and looked out the room's tiny window.

"Listen here, Mr. Deputy," Carpio reacted sarcastically. "With all due respect, why do you have us here with all the dead people?"

"Better to be among the dead than to wake up dead like them, don't you think?"

Carpio didn't utter a peep.

Los hermanos machete

NO TAN ALEGRE COMO los tres Juanes en el cuento anterior, pero divertidos sin embargo son los hermanos machete. Recuerdo el día bien claro. Era un sábado. Acababa de comer y salí a gozar de mi dulce de palito en la sombra. Me senté muy a gusto en la tierra con la espalda contra la pared de nuestro pequeño hogar de adobe. Estiré las piernas. El dulce redondo de naranja que me había comprado el día anterior en la tienda de don Carlos Buenas apenas me cabía en la boca. Poco a poco se hizo más chiquito con cada lamida que le daba.

Mi gozo de buenas a primeras se interrumpió con un estrépito. No sabía de dónde venía. Me tapé una oreja. Oí voces. Me puse de pie y vi al otro lado del callejón (actualmente se llama Martínez Avenue) en la yarda delante de esta casa a dos hombres gritándose. Se echaban de contado, se insultaban, y se amenazaban. En un inesperado momento vi que movían los brazos en el aire y saltaban chispas de dos cuchillotes. Me entró miedo y fui volando a decirle a mamá lo que acababa de ver.

—Amá, amá. Ahi están dos hombres averiguando y echándose malas palabras.

—Vamos a ver. No cuesta nada. Yo te sigo—dijo ella, y salimos para ver por las rendijas del cerco de madera que daba hacia el callejón—. ¡Dios mío! Se van a matar esos idiotas. Mira cómo saltan las chispas de esos machetes. Yo creo que andan borrachos.

—Amá, ¿qué son machetes?

—Oh, hijito. Yo no sé cómo explicártelo. Ve pregúntale a tu papá. Él sabe más de esas cosas. Allá está en casa de tu agüelita.

Fui, toqué la puerta de la cocina, y entré. Ellos estaban bebiendo café y platicando quién sabe de qué.

—Buenas tarde, hijito. ¿Qué vientos te traen por acá?

—Vine a preguntarle algo a papá.

—Y por qué no a mí—dijo ella sonriéndose.

—Apá, ¿qué es un machete?

—Ah, no me digas—interrumpió mi abuelita antes de que respondiera papá —. A poco ya están los hermanos machete con sus machetes.

—¿Pero qué son machetes?—volví a preguntar.

—Todos los sábados por la tarde—continuó mi abuelita—, se emborrachan y salen al patio y chispas vuelan de esos machetes filudos y largos. Se parecen al cuchillo que usa tu agüelito en el rancho para una matanza. Da miedo ver a esos hermanos con sus machetes.

—Agüelita, ¿y qué no se lastiman o se cortan?

—No. Nada de daño. Asina son los borrachos. Tienen más suerte que el diablo.

—¿Pero que estos hermanos no tienen nombres verdaderos?

—Son los Vallejos. Uno se llama Carpio y el otro Plácido. Ellos trabajan en una compañía que se llama Pura Harina (*Purina*). Es donde venden comida pa perros y gatos.

—¿Es por eso que se pelean como perros y gatos agüelita?

—Eso no tiene chiste—intercaló mi papá.

—De todos modos—continuó mi abuelita—, con el dinero que ganan ahi en la Pura Harina es como se compran sus cervezas.

—Pero mamá—añadió mi papá—, ellos están casado, ¿qué no?

—Sí, ahi viven los dos con sus esposas en esa mesma casa que es grande como la mía.

—Pero que yo sepa sus esposas nunca se ven—comentó papá.

—Ah, hijo mío. No te creigas tú eso. Ellas tamién se emborrachan de vez en cuando junto con sus esposos. Salen casi en pelotas, agarrándose de las greñas, y echándose disparates. Tienen unas lenguas que déjate.

—Güeno agüelita, ya me voy. Voy a decirle a mi amá lo que es un machete.

Pues dicho y hecho. Casi todos los sábados por la tarde se oían los machetazos, una que otra palabrota por aquí y por allá, y los disparates de las esposas. Todo ello retumbaba por el callejón.

En Santa Bárbara había un diputado honorario que llevaba por nombre Justín Naranjos. Él y su troquita tenían fama. A él iban los vecinos con quejas acerca de los hermanos machete aunque algunas gentes los veían más bien como algo divertido y no amenazante.

Otro sábado estaba por encima, y el Diputado Naranjos, hombre alto y fuerte, trató de calmar a los hermanos machete pero sin éxito. Harto de los bullicios y las quejas contra Plácido y Carpio echó a cada uno en el cajón de su troquita y los llevó al cementerio de Santa Bárbara donde el diputado era un saca-sepulcros. Los encerró en un cuartito para que pasaran la noche y se les quitara la borrachera. Por la mañana le dio a cada uno su taza de café solo antes de que los dejara irse a casa. No acababan de tomarse el café cuando se puso de pie Carpio y vio hacia fuera por la ventanita del cuarto.

—Oiga Señor Diputao—reaccionó Carpio de una manera sarcástica—. Con todo respeto, ¿por qué nos tiene aquí con todos los muertos?

—Mejor estar entre los muertos que no amanecer muertos como ellos, ¿qué no?

Carpio no dijo ni pío.

Reina

OF ALL THE CHARACTERS depicted in this memoir, no one evokes more love and empathy than Reina, the Queen. Reina, that's what her mother called her. She was fourteen years old and lived with her parents. The family was poor but even more so than the rest of the people in Santa Barbara. Reina and her parents resided in an old railroad car that had been donated to her father by the Santa Fe Railroad Shops, where he worked as a laborer. The car-train, as the neighbors called it, was next to the ditch that ran through the neighborhood.

Reina, like me, attended Santa Barbara School, but she was a few years older. Whether coming or going to school, I saw from afar that she always walked alone. One day, as classes ended, I rushed through a side door and almost tripped over her. She smiled. I saw at that split moment that she was short and a tad stout, with a round face. She struck me as being neither ugly nor pretty.

"Forgive me," she said.

"No, no. It's my fault. I almost knocked you over for running like a jerk," were the first words that popped into my head.

"By the way, my name is Reina. What's yours? Tell me. I won't bite you," and she smiled.

"My name is Junie García. I live . . ."

"I know where you live," she interjected. "I have seen you come out from the little room belonging to doña Emilia García."

"You know my grandma?"

"Yes. She raises chickens that my father buys from her, from time to time. He likes fried chicken very much. Okay, see you later. Oh, by the way. Sometime you must come to meet my parents. We live on this street by the ditch." Her invitation surprised me. We had barely met.

"Why not!" I responded without thinking, and she proceeded down the street. She walked a little ways, glanced back, and waved at me.

Mom was waiting for me under the shade of one of the trees in front of my grandparents' house.

"Who's your girlfriend?" Mom uttered with a smile.

"Her name is Reina. You've seen the railroad car next to the ditch. That's where she lives, this side of don Carlos Buenas's store."

Sooner or later I noticed at school the way that Reina dressed. She wore very nice flowered dresses, but the other girls' clothes were more stylish. Within time I learned that the older women in the vicinity gave Reina their clothes—clothing that they no longer wanted. If not, her mother bought them at a second-hand store near the San Ignacio Church.

Aside from her dresses, Reina also wore high-top shoes like mine, or snake killers as I called them, back in the Río Puerco Valley. I had no other school shoes. And my classmates at Santa Barbara School made fun of me. Perhaps those were the only shoes Reina had as well.

Of course I was dying of curiosity. "Why does she wear high-top shoes all the time?" I asked myself. Little by little I started hearing gossip and murmuring among my schoolmates. I heard ugly stories, some quite rude. It was rumored that she had six toes on each foot. Other gossipmongers claimed that instead of five toes she only had two fat ones, one on each foot. The truth wasn't known for sure because Reina never failed to wear her high-top shoes.

One Saturday morning Mom sent me to buy soap powder for her dishes at don Carlos's store. I went, bought the soap, thanked him, and said good-bye. As I crossed the ditch I heard a voice a little ways off. Then I heard my name.

"Hey, Junie." I saw that it was Reina. She was tossing round rocks that skipped on the water. "Come closer. Are you in a hurry?"

"Yes and no. I came to the store for Mom."

"I want you to meet Dad and Mom. It won't take long," she said, and we went into the railroad car. "Dad, Mom, this is Junie García. He's the grandson of the woman where Dad buys chickens."

"Ah, yes. Good woman," commented the wife. "My husband loves your grandma's chickens."

"I'll be sure to tell her. All right, please excuse me? I have to go help Mom wash dishes."

"Come back anytime," said the mother. "Treat this as your home . . . no, no your train," and she chuckled.

"Thank you very much, ma'am. Okay, I'll see you at school, Reina," I said, and I hurried home.

"Why did you take so long, hijito?" Mom asked. I told her I had seen Reina and that she had invited me to meet her parents.

"Mom, they're really poor but good people. I liked Reina's mom, although her father was a bit quiet."

Within time, Reina and I got to know each other. Now I had a female friend on our street because the rest of the youngsters were boys. I would see her coming or going from school. At times I saw her at the ditch. Whenever Mom sent me to buy something at don Carlos's store, Reina would be tossing small rocks into the water or observing small fish that jumped up from the water.

One day, after I had bought some candy and gum, I saw Reina at the ditch. I stopped by to chitchat with her. She had her feet in the water with her high-top shoes to one side. We chatted for a while, but not for one moment did she stick her feet in and out of the water in a playful way like all the young kids. That caught my attention. I was about to say goodbye when Reina's mother showed up.

"But look what we have here. What a surprise! Look Junie," she said, remembering my name, "this coming Sunday around two o'clock we're going to have a small party here at the house. I want you to join us. We're going to celebrate Reina's birthday."

"Thank you, ma'am. I'll ask my parents to see if I can come. Okay, I'll see you Reina." She waved at me but continued to keep her feet in the water.

That Sunday I dressed up and went to the party. I took a few bizcochitos that Mom had baked. That was my birthday gift for Reina. When I arrived, she and her parents were seated alone at a small table. Delaware Punch and Orange Crush refreshments, along with pastry and turnovers, decorated the table. I felt a bit uneasy and at the same time sad because there were no other guests, but upon seeing Reina dressed up I felt happier. She was wearing a very pretty puffed up pink dress that touched the floor. She wasn't the same Reina I had seen in school or at the ditch with her feet in the water. She truly looked like a queen.

Soon a few guests arrived. Some were Reina's classmates. Shortly thereafter her father extended a warm welcome to everyone.

"Dear guests, welcome to the party! Please have a seat on the floor. That's what those cushions are for. Don't be shy. This is your home. Today is a very special day for Reina. We're here to celebrate her birthday with love and joy. This festivity is called *la quinceañera*. So I'm glad that you have come to observe this special day with me and my wife in honor of our beloved daughter. Now I want to recite these words that I have written in honor of Reina.

Querida Reina.
Hoy que cumples
tus quince años
dejas de ser una niña
y llegas a jovencita.

Te deseo buena suerte
desde hoy en adelante.

Ahora hay que celebrar
este dichoso día contigo.
///
Beloved Reina.
Today you're
fifteen years old
and no longer
a little girl but
rather a young lady.

I wish you
the best of luck
from this day forward.
Now let us celebrate
this happy day with you.

He had barely finished his eloquent words when don Carlos Buenas walked in with a birthday cake and fifteen sparkling candles. He placed the cake delicately on the small table and then unexpectedly burst out singing "Las Mañanitas" in a beautiful and strong voice that echoed throughout Reina's modest home.

Estas son las mañanitas
que cantaba el rey David.
Hoy Reina
por ser día de tu santo
te las canto yo a ti.
///
These are las mañanitas
that King David used to sing.
Today Reina
since it's your saint's day
I'm here to sing them to you.

(Applause)

Everyone, including Reina's mom and dad, accompanied don Carlos, who continued singing.

El día en que tú naciste
nacieron todas las flores.
En la pila del bautismo
cantaron los ruiseñores.
///
On the day you were born
all the flowers were (also) born.
At the baptismal font
the nightingales sang (as well).

(More strong applause)

Reina's mother cut the cake and invited everybody to have a soft drink. After having a good time, the guests congratulated Reina and bid her good-bye. She was in seventh heaven. That Sunday had been the happiest day of her life.

Next day her mom got up early. It was time to wake Reina up so she could have breakfast before departing for school, but she didn't find her in bed. She went to see if Reina was at the outhouse but she wasn't there either. Beside herself, she nudged her husband who was sound asleep.

"Dear, wake up, wake up! It's Reina. I can't find her." He jumped out of bed, got dressed in a flash, and went outside to look for her. She was nowhere around. The neighbors, including the personnel at Santa Barbara School, didn't take long to find out that Reina was missing.

One of those staff members was the coach, Mr. Valerio. On Monday morning, as usual, he had taken a trail that ran alongside the ditch close to where Bobby Herrera and his sister, Irene, lived. As he reached the bend that intersected with the Mother Ditch he saw something suspicious. It resembled a human corpse going round and round in the whirlpool. He took off in a hurry, and ran into the principal's office to tell him what he had seen.

"Goodness gracious! Don't tell me," the principal cried out.

"What? What?" the coach responded.

"Don't tell me that it's Reina. Her father was here a few minutes ago. He came to see if by chance she was here at school."

The principal and the coach took off at a fast pace to the Mother Ditch. What looked like a corpse was still there, going round and round. Without hesitation the principal took off his shoes and shirt and dove into the water. He stopped the body from swirling as best he could and turned it face up.

"Oh dear! What did I tell you!" he shouted in a loud voice. "It's Reina, our student."

The principal and the coach fetched the corpse from the water and placed it at the edge of the ditch. A nightgown and socks were the only things she was wearing. They called the authorities who picked up the body right away before the parents received the sad news.

Reina was in the habit of sleepwalking. This occurred from time to time. Evidently that's what happened that night. She left the house in her sleep and fell—or dove—into the ditch without knowing how to swim, and drowned.

That night a vigil was held for Reina. She was not wearing her high-top shoes or socks. Mourners saw that she didn't have normal feet. Rather, they looked like a solid pair of flesh-and-bone mittens with no toes at all. Her mother approached the body and was heard murmuring to herself in a soft voice. "My beloved daughter, from heaven to earth there are no secrets. Sooner or later everything becomes known. May God look after you in heaven."

La Reina

DE TODOS LOS PERSONAJES representados en estas memorias nadie evoca más amor y empatía que la Reina. La Reina, así la llamaba su mamá. Tenía catorce años y vivía con sus padres. La familia era pobre pero aún más pobre que el resto de la gente de Santa Bárbara. La Reina y sus padres residían en un carro viejo de ferrocarril que le habían regalado al padre en los Shapes de Santa Fe donde él era obrero. El carro-tren, como le llamaban los vecinos, estaba a un lado de la acequia que atravesaba por la vecindad.

La Reina, como yo, asistía a la Escuela de Santa Bárbara, pero ella era unos años mayor. Ya fuera de ida o de vuelta a la escuela, yo veía desde lejos que siempre caminaba a solas. Un día al acabarse las clases rompí corriendo por una puerta del lado de la escuela y por poco tropiezo con ella. Se sonrió ella. Vi en ese dado momento que era bajita y poco gordita con una cara redonda. No me pareció fea ni bonita.

—Perdóname—dijo ella.

—No, no. Es culpa mía. Por poco te tumbo por andar corriendo como un torpe—fueron las primeras palabras que se me vinieron a la cabeza.

—*By the way*, yo me llamo Reina. ¿Cómo te llamas tú? Dime. No te muerdo—y se sonrió.

—Me llamo Junie García. Vivo . . .

—Ya sé dónde vives—intercaló ella—. Yo te he visto salir de aquel cuartito de doña Emilia García.

—¿Tú conoces a mi agüelita?

—Sí. Ella cría gallinas que mi papá le compra de vez en cuando. A él le gusta mucho la gallina frita. Bueno, nos vemos. Oh, *by the way*. Alguna vez tendrás que venir para que conozcas a mis padres. Vivimos en esta calle a un lado de la acequia—. Su invitación me sorprendió. Apenas nos habíamos conocido.

—¡Cómo que no!—le respondí sin pensar, y ella siguió calle abajo. Anduvo poco trecho, echó una mirada hacia atrás, y me capeó con la mano.

Mamá estaba esperándome bajo la sombra de uno de los árboles delante de la casa de mis abuelitos.

—¿Quién es tu novia?—. Mamá prorrumpió con una risita.

—Se llama Reina. Tú has visto el carro de tren al lado de la 'cequia. Ahi vive, de este lado de la tienda de don Carlos Buenas.

Tarde o temprano me di cuenta en la escuela la forma en que la Reina se vestía. Llevaba puestos túnicos muy bonitos con flores, pero las otras muchachas se vestían más de moda. Con el tiempo oí decir que a la Reina le regalaban su ropa las ancianas de la vecindad, ropa que ellas ya no querían. Si no, su mamá se la compraba en una tienda de segunda mano que estaba cerca de la Iglesia de San Ignacio.

Aparte de sus túnicos, la Reina también calzaba zapatos altos como los míos, o mata-víboras como los llamaba yo en mi Valle del Río Puerco. Yo no tenía otros zapatos para la escuela. Y los escueleros en Santa Bárbara se burlaban de mí. Tal vez eran los únicos zapatos que tenía la Reina misma.

Claro que yo me moría de curiosidad. "¿Por qué es que ella siempre calza zapatos altos?" Me pregunté. Poco a poco oí el chismoteo y cuchicheo entre algunos escueleros. Oí cuentos feos, algunos bastante groseros. Se decía que tenía seis dedos en cada pie. Otros mitoteros reclamaban que en vez de cinco dedos ella apenas tenía dos dedos gordos, uno en cada pie. La verdad no se sabía por cierto porque la Reina nunca dejaba de calzar sus zapatos altos.

Un sábado por la mañana me despachó mamá a que le comprara

jabón en polvo para los trastes en la tienda de don Carlos. Fui, compré el jabón, le di las gracias, y me despedí. Al cruzar la acequia oí una voz un poco a lo lejos. Luego oí mi nombre.

—¡Eh, Junie!—. Vi que era la Reina. Estaba tirando rodajas de piedras que daban saltos por el agua. —Acércate. ¿Estás apurado?

—Sí y no. Vine a la tienda pa mi amá.

—Quiero que conozcas a papá y a mamá—dijo ella—. No tarda mucho—y entramos en el carro ferrocarril—. Papá, mamá, éste es Junie García. Es el nieto de la mujer donde compra papá gallinas.

—Ah, sí. Buena señora—comentó la esposa—. A mi esposo le encanta la carne de gallina de tu abuela.

—Ya se lo digo. Güeno, descúlpenme por favor. Tengo que ir ayudarle a mi amá lavar los trastes.

—Vuelve cuando gustes—dijo la madre—. Aquí tienes tu casa . . . no, no, tu tren—y soltó una risita.

—Munchas gracias señora. Güeno, te veo en la escuela Reina—le dije y me apuré a casa.

—¿Por qué te tardates, hijito?—. Preguntó mamá. Le conté que vi a la Reina y que ella me convidó a que conociera a sus padres.

—Amá, ellos son pobrecitos pero güena gente. Me gustó la mamá de la Reina aunque su papá era un poco callado.

Con el tiempo nos conocimos más la Reina y yo. Ahora tenía yo una amiga en nuestra calle porque los demás jóvenes eran muchachos. Yo la veía yendo o viniendo de la escuela. A veces la veía en la acequia cuando me despachaba mamá a comprar algo en la tienda de don Carlos. Allí estaba la Reina tirando piedritas en el agua u observando a los pescaditos que saltaban del agua.

Un día después que compré unos dulces y chicle, vi a la Reina en la acequia. Me detuve a platicar con ella. Tenía los pies en el agua y sus zapatos altos a un lado. Platicamos un rato, pero ella ni por un dado momento metía y sacaba los pies del agua de una manera juguetona como hacía toda la plebe. Eso me llamó la atención. Yo estaba por despedirme cuando se presentó la mamá de la Reina.

—Pero qué tenemos aquí. ¡Qué sorpresa! Mira Junie—dijo

recordando mi nombre—, el domingo que viene a eso de las dos de la tarde vamos a tener una fiestecita aquí en casa. Quiero que nos acompañes. Vamos a celebrar el cumpleaños de la Reina.

—Gracias señora. Les pido permiso a mis padres pa ver si puedo venir. Güeno, nos vemos Reina—. Me saludó ella pero siguió con los pies en el agua.

Ese domingo me vestí bien pantera y fui a la fiesta. Llevé unos bizcochitos que había preparado mamá. Ése fue mi regalo para el cumpleaños de la Reina. Cuando llegué estaban sentados solitos en una mesita ella y sus padres. Refrescos *Delaware Punch* y *Orange Crush*, empanaditas, y pastelitos decoraban la mesa. Me sentí un poco inquieto y a la vez triste porque no había otros huéspedes pero al ver a la Reina bien vestida me sentí más contento. Ella llevaba puesto un vestido esponjado muy bonito color de rosa que daba al suelo. No era la misma Reina que yo había visto en la escuela o en la acequia con los pies en el agua. De veras que parecía una reina.

Dentro de poco llegaron unos invitados. Algunos eran compañeros de clase de la Reina. Dentro de poco nos dio su papá la bienvenida a todos.

—Queridos invitados. ¡Bien venidos a la fiesta! Siéntense en el suelo, por favor. Para eso son esos cojines. No tengan vergüenza. Están en su casa. Hoy es un día muy especial para la Reina. Vamos a celebrar su cumpleaños con amor y gozo. Esta celebración lleva por nombre la quinceañera. Así que me da gusto que hayan venido a festejar este día especial conmigo y mi esposa en honor de nuestra querida hija. Ahora quiero recitar estas palabras que yo he escrito en honor de la Reina.

Querida Reina.
Hoy que cumples
tus quince años
dejas de ser una niña,
y llegas a jovencita.

Te deseo buena suerte
desde hoy en adelante.
Ahora hay que celebrar
este dichoso día contigo.

Apenas acababa sus palabras elogiosas cuando entró don Carlos Buenas con un queque y quince velas brillantes. Colocó el queque con cuidado sobre la mesita y luego inesperadamente estalló cantando "Las Mañanitas" en una linda y fuerte voz que retumbaba por toda el hogar sencillo de la Reina.

Estas son las mañanitas
que cantaba el rey David.
Hoy Reina
por ser día de tu santo
te las canto yo a ti.

(Aplausos)

Todos, incluso el papá y la mamá de Reina, acompañaron a don Carlos que siguió cantando.

El día en que tú naciste
nacieron todas las flores.
En la pila del bautismo
cantaron los ruiseñores.

(Más aplausos fuertes)

Rebanó el queque la mamá de la Reina e invitó a todos a tomar refrescos. Tras pasar un buen rato, los huéspedes felicitaron a la Reina y se despidieron. Ella estaba por las nubes. Ese domingo había sido el día más feliz de su vida.

Al día siguiente se levantó temprano su mamá. Era hora de despertar a la Reina para que desayunara antes de irse a la escuela, pero no la halló en la cama. Fue a ver si estaba la Reina en el escusao pero tampoco se encontraba allí. Fuera de sí, despertó a su marido que estaba bien dormido.

—Querido, ¡despierta, despierta! La Reina. No la hallo—. Saltó de la cama, se vistió en un decir amén, y salió a buscarla. No se encontraba en ningún sitio. Los vecinos, incluso el personal de la escuela de Santa Bárbara, no tardaron en saber que la Reina había desaparecido.

Uno de esos empleados fue el entrenador el Sr. Valerio. El lunes por la mañana pescó como siempre por una vereda que corría a un lado de la acequia cerca de donde vivían Bobby Herrera y su hermana Irene. Al llegar al recodo que pegaba con la Acequia Madre vio algo sospechoso. Parecía un cuerpo humano dándose vueltas y vueltas en un remolino de agua. Partió corriendo y entró en la oficina del principal para decirle lo que había visto.

—¡Dios mío! No me digas—exclamó el principal.

—¿Qué? ¿Qué?—reaccionó el entrenador.

—No me digas que es la Reina. Su papá estuvo aquí hace unos minutos. Vino a ver si por casualidad estaba ella aquí en la escuela.

El principal y el entrenador arrancaron a un paso ligero para la Acequia Madre. Lo que parecía un cadáver todavía estaba allí dándose vueltas y vueltas. Sin vacilar el principal se quitó los zapatos y la camisa y se tiró en el agua. Detuvo el cuerpo lo mejor que pudo para que no siguiera dándose vueltas y lo volteó boca arriba.

—¡Madre mía! ¡Qué te dije!— gritó en voz alta—. Es la Reina, nuestra estudiante.

El principal y el entrenador sacaron el cuerpo del agua y lo colocaron al bordo de la acequia. El camisón y las medias era lo único que llevaba puesto. Llamaron en seguida a las autoridades las cuales recogieron el cuerpo antes de que los padres recibieran las malas noticias.

La Reina tenía la costumbre de caminar en su sueño. Esto ocurría de vez en cuando. Por lo visto es lo que sucedió esa noche. Salió de casa sonámbula y se cayó—o se tiró—en la acequia sin saber cómo nadar y se ahogó.

Esa noche velaron a la Reina. No llevaba puestos sus zapatos altos o medias. Vieron los dolientes que ella no tenía pies normales sino que se asemejaban a dos manoplas de carne y hueso sin dedos del todo. La madre se acercó al cuerpo y se oyó que murmuraba para sí en voz baja estas palabras. "Querida hija mía. Del cielo a la tierra no se guardan secretos. Tarde o temprano todo se sabe. Que Dios te guarde en la gloria."

The Lady with the Goiter

LAST NIGHT I WASN'T able to sleep the whole night through. I kept thinking of Reina. Plus I had one nightmare after another. I dreamt that the deceased from the Santa Barbara Cemetery kept tugging at my feet. Not only that, my little brother Beltrán—who sleeps in the same bed with me—snored like a frog and tossed and turned.

Though today was Friday there was no school. Days like today, Mom as a rule let me sleep in provided I didn't forget to put cotton in my ears so as not to awaken when she got up. If I forgot, I covered my head with my pillow.

Mom awoke very early to fix breakfast for Dad and to prepare his lunch before he left to go work. She saw that I was awake, seated on the bed with my arms resting on my pillow.

"Hijito. What are you doing up with the chickens? Did you forget that there's no school today?"

"I didn't forget, Mom, but Beltrán—Mr. Loose Legs—kicked me all night long and I wasn't able to sleep." I didn't dare tell her about Reina.

"Good gracious! Is that why you're cranky? Okay, I'll heat up some water for your oatmeal and you can eat breakfast with your father."

"Thanks, Mom."

"And later I want you to run an errand for me. I'm going to bake bread today for us to take to the ranch tomorrow but I've run out of baking powder."

"Mom, I didn't know we were going to the ranch. That's great! I'll be able to see and ride Bayo and Prieto."

"Come now, eat. Your horses will wait for you, but your oatmeal's getting cold."

Dad finished eating, gave Mom a hug, and left for work. Little by little Beltrán, Juanito, and Julianita got up. Elsie, the baby who slept with my parents, was still asleep. One by one they ate breakfast while I waited for the big hand on the clock to strike twelve and the little one, eight. At precisely eight o'clock is when don Carlos, where I generally went on food errands, opened his store.

"Did you finish eating breakfast?" Mom asked me. "Ah, I see that you left your bowl squeaky clean like a cat," and she winked at me. "Here's four bits," she said, and she gave me two two-bit coins, one in each hand. "Buy me a small can of baking powder; you already know the brand. I also need yeast . . . and don't go to don Carlos's store. Go to the Moyas' corner store. It's closer."

I put the two quarters in the leather coin purse that Dad had given me. I didn't take long to get to the Moyas' store. It was really close—at the end of the street where we lived, on the opposite side of don Carlos's store. It was my first visit. I went in with my eyes wide open and full of curiosity. As I entered I saw this tall man with glasses behind a wooden counter. What caught my eye also was a glass cabinet with all kinds of tobacco. It reminded me of Ruppe's Drugstore on south Fourth Street in Albuquerque where Grandpa Lolo bought cigars and herbal remedies.

"Good morning, kid. I haven't seen you before. You're new around here, huh," the gentleman commented.

"More or less. I've been living on this street for almost a year."

"What's your name?"

"Junie. Junie García. I'm doña Emilia's grandson."

"Don't tell me. I know who she is. She comes by here once in a while on her return from Mass, above all during Holy Week. She stops to purchase yeast to bake bread on Good Friday."

"That's why I came, for yeast, but not for Grandma. For my mom. She asked me to buy a little package. I also need a small can of baking powder."

"I only have one kind of yeast, but two kinds of baking powder. Which one do you want?" he asked, and he pointed at the shelves next to the counter.

"That one—the black-and-red can with the letters KC."

At that moment this lady came in. The first thing that caught my eye were her muscular arms. Then I saw her neck. I couldn't help but see that she had a fairly large goiter. I had never seen anything like it. The only similar thing was the dewlap of my aunt Taida's turkey at the ranch.

"Good morning, doña Terencia," came the cordial greeting from Mrs. Moya. "How are you this morning?"

"Alive and kicking, thank God."

"What can I do for you today?"

"Well today is Friday. The usual. Three small packages of yeast, please."

"We only have two, nothing more. I've just sold one to this boy," said Mrs. Moya, and the woman just kept staring at me.

"What's your name?" she asked me with an unperturbed look, as if I had committed a crime or done something wrong.

"Junie García."

"And where do you live?"

"At my grandma's storage shed on this street."

"And who's your grandmother?"

"Doña Emilia García," I answered formally.

"Ah, nice person. She raises baby chicks and when they're grown she gives some of them to poor people in the community. May God safeguard a precious place in heaven for her," she exclaimed with a more sensitive and humane gesture than the one she had treated me with previously. In any case, her goiter piqued my curiosity more than her flattery.

I returned home as quickly as I could. I was anxious to tell Mom about the lady with the goiter. I dashed in, almost out of breath, and I put the yeast and the baking powder on top of the table.

"Mom! Mom! Guess what!"

"Don't tell me. The world is soon coming to an end," she remarked jokingly.

Mom was already accustomed to my returning home with something remarkable or unexpected that had occurred to me on one of my errands.

"No, Mom. I saw this lady who went to buy yeast."

"And that's why you dashed in here like a whirlwind? Didn't you yourself go there to buy yeast?"

"Yes, but this woman has a goiter the size of a cantaloupe. I have never seen anything like it. I didn't know what to think. I got scared and at the same time felt pity."

"Ah, that must be doña Terencia."

"Yes, that's her name. She knows Grandma. But why does she have that goiter that hangs practically down to her chest?"

"I don't know why. No doubt it comes from an illness that she suffered."

"I'm going to ask my grandma. Let's see what she tells me."

"Come in, come in. Wasn't there any school today?" was the first thing my grandma asked.

"No. The teachers had something or other to do. Grandma, I have a question."

"Only one! Well let's see."

"I went to get yeast for Mom at the Moyas'. In walked this woman with a huge goiter. And not only that, she had these really fat arms."

"Hijito, that's doña Terencia. She's well-known in the vicinity. And . . ."

"Because of her goiter, Grandma?" I interrupted.

"Yes and no. When someone says 'the lady with the goiter,' everybody knows whom they're talking about. But look, hijito, she's known not due to her physical problem but because of the delicious bread that she bakes—above all, during Christmas or Holy Week. People already know, the women more than anyone else, where the aroma comes from that makes your mouth water. Many neighbors go there to buy her loaves of bread. At times you'll even see a line of people outside her home."

"And where does this woman live?"

"On this street behind the Moyas' store. You can almost see the house from here."

"A curious thing, Grandma: she also went to buy yeast this morning."

"Well it won't be long before the bread aroma starts spewing from her stovepipe. You'll see what I'm talking about."

"And do you know how much she sells her loaves of bread for?"

"I understand that it depends on the size. Fifteen or twenty cents. That's how she earns a little money to help support herself and her husband. He's not able to work."

"What's wrong with him? Is he old or what?"

"It's not that. The poor soul has mental problems. He can't remember one thing from one day to the next. Hijito, when the mind is not sound, the body suffers. It's sad."

"Okay, I'm off. If I smell doña Terencia's bread today or tomorrow I'll ask Mom for money to buy me a loaf before we leave for the ranch. That way she doesn't have to bake bread," I said, and I returned home.

"Well, what good news do you bring me now?" Mom asked.

"Mom, Grandma says that doña Terencia is known more for her bread than her goiter. Above all, during Christmas and Holy Week. That's how she and her husband survive because he's sick in the head. He's nuts."

"Hijito, don't say that about the poor man."

That Friday afternoon I went to get water for Mom from my grandparents' pump. As I pumped water the bread aroma struck me. Surely it had to be coming from doña Terencia's home. I informed Mom about it.

"Mom. You can smell doña Terencia's bread. Can I go buy a loaf?"

"Do you have money?" She knew very well that I didn't have a cent.

"Nothing, nothing. Not even a penny."

"Well, ask your father. If he gives you some then I won't have to bake bread after supper to take to the ranch."

Dad gave me two bits. When I got to doña Terencia's house there were several people waiting outside the kitchen. It took a little time for me to go in. Right away, doña Terencia recognized me, but this time I looked more at her face and not her thick arms or melon-sized goiter. She looked happy selling her bread.

"What a pleasure to see you, Junie!" were her first words, which pleased me—especially since she had remembered my name. "How can I help you? No, no. Don't tell me. I bet I can guess why you came. Bread!" And she laughed from cheek to cheek.

"Yes. I have two bits that my father gave me. What size bread can you sell me?"

"Look. I'm going to give you two loaves. The small one's for you and the large one for the rest of your family. Here," she said, and she put one loaf in each hand. "I've just got them out of the oven. They're still quite warm."

"Thanks very much, doña Terencia." As I got to the door she called me back.

"Wait just a second."

"Yes, ma'am."

She fetched a large jar from the dish cupboard. It was practically full of tiny balls of all colors. God knows what they were. They looked like my marbles. She removed the jar's lid, stuck a hand inside, and took out a ball.

"Open your mouth, hijito,"and she put one on my tongue. "Chew it! It's gum." I went home happy and at a fast pace. I didn't want the bread to get cold.

Saturday, we went to the ranch and returned Sunday evening. On Monday afternoon upon returning from school, I stopped by doña Terencia's house. I knocked on the door.

"Ah, what a surprise! I'm happy to see you, Junie."

"I came to tell you that the loaves of bread that you sold me were really tasty. My family and I liked them."

"I'm glad you enjoyed them."

I walked home slowly thinking about doña Terencia, the lady with the goiter, whose bread brings joy to endless people's palates in the community. I also liked the gum she gave me.

La mujer del buche

ANOCHE NO PUDE DORMIR la noche entera. No dejaba de pensar en la Reina. Además, tuve una pesadilla tras otra. Soñé que los difuntos del Cementerio de Santa Bárbara no dejaban de jalarme los pies. No sólo eso, mi hermanito Beltrán que duerme en la mesma cama conmigo roncó como una rana y se dio vueltas y vueltas.

Aunque hoy era viernes no hubo escuela. Días como éste mamá por lo general me dejaba guardar cama con tal de que no se me olvidara ponerme motas de algodón en los oídos para no despertar cuando ella se levantara. Si se me olvidaba me tapaba la cabeza con mi almohada.

Mamá despertó tempranito para hacerle desayuno a papá y prepararle su lonche antes de irse él a trabajar. Vio ella que yo estaba despierto, sentado en la cama con los brazos recostados sobre mi almohada.

—Hijito. ¿Qué haces tan temprano como las gallinas? ¿Qué se te olvidó que hoy no tienes escuela?

—No se me olvidó amá, pero el patas sueltas de Beltrán me pataleó toda la noche y no pude dormir. No me atreví a decirle lo de la Reina.

—¡Válgame Dios! Por eso amanecites muino. Güeno, te caliento agua pa que hagas aveno y almuerces con tu papá.

—Gracias amá.

—Y más tarde quiero que me hagas un mandado. Voy hacer pan

hoy pa llevarnos nosotros al rancho mañana pero se me acabó la espauda.

—Amá, yo no sabía que íbanos al rancho. ¡Qué güeno! Podré ver y pasearme en Bayo y el Prieto.

—Anda, come. Tus caballos te esperan, pero el aveno se te está enfriando.

Acabó de comer papá, le dio un abrazo a mamá, y se fue al trabajo. Poco a poco se fueron levantando Beltrán, Juanito, y Julianita. Mi hermanita Elsie, la niña que dormía con mis padres, todavía no recordaba. Desayunaron uno por uno mientras yo esperaba a que la aguja grande del reloj pegara con el número doce y la chiquita con el ocho. A las meras ocho era cuando abría su tienda don Carlos a donde iba yo generalmente de mandados.

—¿Ya acabates de almorzar?—me preguntó mamá—. Ah, veo que dejates la olla limpiecita como un gato—y me hizo un guiño—. Aquí tienes cuatro reales—y me puso dos monedas de dos reales, una en cada mano—. Me compras un botito de espauda, ya tú sabes la marca. Tamién necesito levadura . . . y no vayas a la tienda de don Carlos. Vete a la tiendita de los señores Moya. Está más cerca.

Puse los cuatro reales en el guarda monedas que me había regalado papá. No tardé en llegar a la tienda de los Moya. Estaba bien cerquita, a fines de la calle donde vivíamos al lado opuesto de la tienda de don Carlos. Era mi primera visita. Entré con los ojos bien abiertos y lleno de curiosidad. Al entrar vi a este hombre alto con anteojos detrás de un mostrador de madera. Lo que me llamó la atención también fue un armario de cristal con toda clase de tabacos. Me hizo recordar de la Botica Ruppe en la Calle Cuarta en la Plaza (Alburquerque) donde compraba puros y remedios mi abuelito Lolo.

—Buenos días, jovencito. No te he visto antes. Eres nuevo por acá, eh—comentó el señor.

—Más o menos. Hace cuasi un año que vivo en esta calle.

—¿Cómo te llamas?

—Junie. Junie García. Soy nieto de doña Emilia García.

—No me digas. Sé quién es. Ella pasa por aquí de vez en cuando al regresar de misa, sobre todo durante la Semana Santa. Viene a comprar levadura para hacer pan los Viernes Santos.

—Por eso vine yo, por levadura, pero no pa mi agüelita. Pa mi amá. Me mandó que comprara un parquetito. Tamién necesito un bote chico de espauda.

—Levadura tengo solamente una clase, pero espauda hay dos marcas. ¿Cuál quieres?—me preguntó, y las señaló en la estantería a un lado del mostrador.

—Ésa—la del bote negro y colorado con las letras KC.

En eso entró esta señora. Lo primero que me llamó la atención fueron aquellos brazos macizos que tenía. Luego vi su pescuezo. No pude menos de ver que tenía un buche bastante grande. Jamás había visto tal cosa. Lo único parecido era la papada del torque de mi tía Taida en el rancho.

—Buenos días doña Terencia—saludo cordial de la señora Moya—. ¿Cómo amaneció?

—Bien. Pataleando pero viva gracias a Dios.

—¿Qué se le ofrece hoy?

—Pues hoy es viernes. Lo de siempre. Tres parquetitos de levadura, por favor.

—Nos quedan dos, nada más. Acabo de venderle uno a este muchacho—dijo la señora Moya, y se quedó mirándome la mujer.

—¿Cómo te llamas tú?—me preguntó con una cara impávida como si yo hubiera cometido un crimen o hecho algo malo.

—Junie García.

—¿Y dónde vives tú?

—En la dispensa de mi agüelita en esta calle.

—¿Y quién es tu abuela?

—Doña Emilia García—le respondí de una manera formal.

—Ah, buena gente. Ella cría pollitos y cuando crecen regala parte de ellos a gente pobre en la comunidad. Que Dios le guarde un lugar precioso en la gloria—exclamó con gesto más sensitivo y humano del cual me trató a mí anteriormente. De todas formas, su buche me llamó más la atención que sus halagos.

Regresé a casa tan pronto como pude. Me daban ansias por contarle a mamá de la mujer con el buche. Entré volando, casi sin resuello, y puse la levadura y la espauda sobre la mesa.

—¡Amá! ¡Amá! ¿Sabes qué?

—No me digas. A poco ya viene la finación del mundo—dijo como chiste.

Mamá ya estaba impuesta a que yo retornara a casa con algo extraordinario o inesperado que me había acontecido en uno de mis mandados.

—No, amá. Vi a esta mujer que jue a comprar levadura.

—¿Y por eso entrates como un remolino? ¿Qué no juites tú mesmo allá a comprar levadura?

—Sí, pero esta señora tenía un buche del tamaño diun melón roñoso. Jamás había visto tal cosa. No supe qué pensar. Me dio miedo y a la mesma vez lástima.

—Ah, tiene que ser doña Terencia.

—Sí, asina se llama. Ella conoce a mi agüelita. ¿Pero por qué tiene ese buche que le cuelga cuasi hasta al pecho?

—No sé por qué. Seguro que viene de una enfermedá que tuvo.

—Yo voy a preguntarle a mi agüelita. A ver qué me dice ella.

—Entra, entra. ¿Qué no hubo escuela hoy?—fue lo primero que me preguntó.

—No. Las mestras tenían no sé qué. Agüelita, tengo una pregunta.

—¡Apenas una! Pues vamos a ver.

—Jui por levadura pa mamá en la tienda de los Moya. Entró esta mujer con un buche grandote. Y no solamente eso, tenía unos brazos pero bien gordos.

—Hijito. Es doña Terencia. Ella se conoce bien en la vecindad. Y . . .

—¿Por su buche, agüelita?—interrumpí yo.

—Sí y no. Cuando alguien dice "la mujer del buche," todo el

mundo sabe de quién se habla. Pero mira hijito, ella tiene fama no por su malestar físico sino por el sabroso pan que cocina sobre todo durante la Navidad o en la Semana Santa. La gente ya sabe, las mujeres más que naide, de dónde viene l'aroma que le hace a uno agua la boca. Allí van muchos vecinos a comprar sus tortas de pan. A veces hasta se ve un chorro de personas fuera de su casa.

—¿Y dónde vive esta mujer?

—En esta calle detrás de la tienda de los Moya. Casi se ve la casa desde aquí.

—Cosa curiosa, agüelita. Ella tamién jue a comprar levadura esta mañana.

—Pues tardará poco pa que l'aroma del pan salga por el chiflón de su estufa. Ya verás lo que te digo.

—¿Y usté sabe por cuánto vende las tortas de pan?

—Tengo entendido que depende del tamaño. Por quince o veinte centavos. Asina es como gana su dinerito pa mantenerse ella y su marido. Él no puede trabajar.

—¿Qué tiene? ¿Está viejito o qué?

—No es eso. El pobrecito padece de la mente. No se acuerda de las cosas de un día a otro. Hijito, cuando la mente no está sana, el cuerpo padece. Da lástima.

—Güeno, ya me voy. Si huelo el pan de doña Terencia hoy o mañana le pido dinero a mi amá pa comprarme una torta antes de irnos al rancho. Asina no tiene que hacer pan ella—y regresé a casa.

—¿Pues qué güenas nuevas me traes ora?—preguntó mamá.

—Amá. Dice mi agüelita que doña Terencia se conoce más por sus panes y no por el buche. Más que nada pa la Navidad y la Semana Santa. Asina se mantienen ella y su esposo porque él está mal de la cabeza. Le falta una tuerca.

—Hijito. No digas eso del pobre hombre.

Ese viernes por la tarde fui a sacar agua pa mamá de la pompa de mis abuelitos. Al pompear agua me pegó el aroma de pan. Sin duda que venía de la casa de doña Terencia. Le avisé a mamá.

—Amá. Se huele el pan de doña Terencia. ¿Puedo ir a comprar una torta?

—¿Tú tienes dinero?—. Ella sabía muy bien que yo no tenía ni un centavo.

—Nada, nada. Ni siquiera un pene.

—Pues pídele a tu papá. Si te da con qué entonces no tengo que hacer pan después de la cena pa llevar al rancho.

Papá me dio dos reales Cuando llegué a casa de doña Terencia había varias personas esperando fuera de la cocina. Tardé poco en entrar. En seguida me reconoció doña Terencia, pero esta vez me fijé más en su cara y no en los brazos gruesos o el buche tamaño de un melón. Ella se veía contenta vendiendo su pan.

—¡Qué gusto me da en verte Junie—fueron las primeras palabras lo cual me agradó ya que recordó mi nombre—. ¿En qué puede ayudarte? No, no. No me digas. A que te adivino por qué viniste. ¡Por pan!—y sonrió de cachete a cachete.

—Sí. Aquí tengo dos reales que me dio en papá. ¿Qué tamaño de pan me puede vender?

—Mira. Te voy a dar dos piezas. La chiquita es para ti y la grande para el resto de tu familia. Toma—me dijo y puso una torta en cada mano—. Acabo de sacarlas del horno de la estufa. Todavía están calientitas.

—Munchas gracias, doña Terencia—. Al salir de la puerta me llamó.

—Espérate un momentito.

—Sí señora.

Sacó del trastero un frasco grande. Estaba casi lleno de bolitas de todos colores. Sabrá Dios qué serían. Se parecían a mis canicas. Le quitó la tapadera al frasco, metió una mano, y sacó una bolita.

—Abre la boca hijito—y me puso una en la lengua—. ¡Máscatela! Es chicle—. Me fui a casa alegre y a un paso rápido. No quería que no se enfriara el pan.

El sábado nos fuimos al rancho y regresamos el domingo por la tarde. El lunes por la tarde al volver a casa de la escuela, paré por la casa de doña Terencia. Toqué la puerta.

—¡Ah qué sorpresa! Me da gusto en verte Junie.

—Vine a decirle que las tortas de pan que me vendió estuvieron murre sabrosas. A mi familia y a mí nos gustaron.

—Me alegro que les gustaran.

Me fui a casa despacito pensando en doña Terencia, la del buche cuyo pan da gusto al paladar de un sinfín de gente en la comunidad. Tamién me gustó el chíquete que me dio.

Spitting Rainbows

PAT PEREA LIVED A few houses from us and near doña Terencia's house. He and I became good friends after a year at Santa Barbara. At times he would stop for me to walk together to class. We were in the same grade at Santa Barbara School.

One day after class, Pat accompanied me home. I had my books and lunch pail, but he wasn't carrying anything. We exchanged lots of silly stuff as he kicked a pebble here and there on the dirt road. We came to the front of the yard where I lived.

"Catch you later," said Pat. "Till tomorrow. I have to go help my old man in the garage," and Pat took off. Then he turned around. "Oh, by the way, would you like to come work your balls off with me sometime? My father and two uncles of mine fix cars that have been in a wreck."

I understood some words, but the rest of his gobbledygook left me scratching my head.

"Work your balls off. What's that?" I asked him.

"To bust your butt," he answered, as though I was supposed to know what he was saying.

"And what do you do?"

"Everything!" he responded, in a vague sort of a way.

"And do you work for nothing or does your dad pay you?"

"You betcha, dude. I'm part of the business that he and my uncles have. With the 'bread' that I earn, I can go to a flick or whatever. What do you say? If you want to I can ask my old man if you can work with me. We can sweat together, you and me."

"Let me talk to my parents. Let's see what they say. I'll let you know tomorrow."

That evening at supper I told Mom and Dad about the job with Pat's father and his uncles. The first thing Dad asked was, "Are they going to pay you?"

"Yes, but I don't know how much."

"Very well, as long as they pay it's okay with me. You're not going to do it for free," and Dad looked at Mom, who agreed.

The next day I ran into Pat on the way to school.

"Hey there! What do you have to say about the job?"

"My parents gave me permission. When can I start?"

"This Friday after school, if you're not busy. I already spoke with my old man."

Before I knew it, Friday was here. Pat accompanied me home after class.

"I'll see you later at my pad so you can meet my old man," Pat said, and he took off.

I went home and after seeing Mom, I changed clothes to chop wood or pump water for her. It didn't take me long.

"I'm ready, Mom. I'm going to see Pat's father. I'll see what kind of work he wants me to do."

"Be careful, hijito," Mom cautioned me. "And be back by suppertime before your dad gets here."

Upon arriving at Pat's house, he was waiting for me on the house porch, rocking in his father's chair.

"Hey there! Boy, but you got here fast."

"Yes, but I have to get back before supper. Something else: Is it okay if I call you Patricio? I have a cousin in Bernalillo with the same name."

"Fine with me. That's what they call me at home. Pat's the name the broads gave me at school."

"Yes, I heard some girls during recess laughing at your name. They were saying Pee, Pee in place of Pat Perea, just to make fun of you. I know what that means. It's not very nice."

"I know who those chicks are. They moved to Martíneztown from San Jo. They can suck my dick," Pat shouted. "Let's go. I want you to meet my old man," and we entered a medium-sized room. The first thing I saw was a small sign on the wall that read Mike's Paint and Body Shop. In a corner, sitting behind a small table, wearing a cap and mask around his neck, was this man. He stood up when he saw us. He was short and a tad obese.

"Dad," said Patricio, "this is Junie García. He's in school with me and lives close by. He's going to help me sweep and clean up the garages."

"Very well, but I don't want any monkey business and you getting hurt," he warned us.

He had quite a large garage with two doors that opened and closed like an accordion, one to one side and the other door to the other side. Patricio and I entered. He showed me the enormous garage. Inside there was a black curtain made of very fine cloth that divided the garage in half.

"This is the first garage. This is where my uncle Cristóbal, my father's brother, repairs cars they bring to Dad that have been in a wreck. Some come with dented doors or fenders. My uncle Cristóbal knows how to straighten them out. Afterward he applies primer, and then after the primer dries it's my turn. I sand the doors or fenders with sandpaper before my uncle Bernardo or my dad paints them to match the rest of the car. They paint them in the second garage. The cars come out looking brand new."

"But what am I going to do, Patricio?"

"Besides sweeping the garages, you and I are going to sandpaper the cars' doors or the parts that are dented. You'll see. I'll show you how. We'll start tomorrow, Saturday. Come in the morning."

That Saturday, since there was no school, I was able to sleep a little late. After eating two slices of Rainbo toast and a small bowl of oatmeal with raisins, I put on my old clothes that I wore to chop wood and do other household chores. I bid Mom and Dad good-bye and took off walking to the Pereas' home. I knocked on the porch. Patricio came out.

"Here I am," I said, and we headed for the first garage. His uncle Cristóbal was already there.

"Good morning, boys. Ready to work?" These were his first words.

"Ready!" we both responded at the same time in a loud voice.

"This car came to us yesterday and as you can see, it was dented on this side from front to back. I already took out the dents and applied the primer. Now it's your turn to work," Patricio's uncle said, and he smiled. "You have to sand the dents with sandpaper until they are smooth. Then the dents are painted to match the rest of the car. That's what my brother Bernardo does or Patricio's father. Okay, Patricio, show your friend how the work is done," advised don Cristóbal.

"It's easy," said Patricio. "I'll start with the fender and you with the door. Look at how I do it. First you start with the roughest sandpaper and you finish with the fine one. Here's both. You sand from one side to the other and then from top to bottom. The fender, as my uncle Cristóbal said, has to be quite smooth."

"Have you done this before?"

"Since last summer. I'm an expert," Patricio confirmed with a wry smile.

We began. I did as Patricio asked me to do. It took me a good while. I sanded and sanded the door, first with the sandy paper, and then I finished with the smooth one. I stroked the door softly with my right hand; it turned out really smooth.

"There you are, Patricio. I'm done. What do you think?" and he looked at my work as though he were my boss.

"*A toda eme*. Out of sight!"

"And what does that mean?"

"*A toda madre*. Like all get out!"

"I'm glad," I answered, although I didn't understand a thing he said. "Okay, Patricio. I have to go. Look at the clock on the wall. It's almost twelve o'clock. Mom told me to get home for lunch."

"Don't forget," Patricio reminded me, "we still have the rear fender. I'll see you this afternoon."

"Good. I'll be back about one, one thirty."

I hurried home to tell Mom about my work. Dad had to work that Saturday morning; he still wasn't back. I dashed in without holding the screen door.

"Ah, hijito. I'm glad to see you. But look at those dirty hands. How was your job?"

"I liked it. I sandpapered a car's door that was in a wreck. That's why my hands are so dirty. We still have part of the car to do. We'll finish it this afternoon, Patricio and I. I told him I'd be back about one o'clock or so. Is that okay, Mom?"

"You'll have to see what your dad says. He's almost back from work. Come. Wash those hands before you eat."

I had barely sat down when Dad walked in. All three of us sat down to eat. Mom had a potato-and-beef stew that she had warmed up. While we ate I asked Dad if I could go work with Patricio that afternoon.

"You may, but don't forget that you have to chop wood for your mom when you get back. Don't put it off till Sunday."

"Okay. I'll be back by five." I finished eating and went to see Patricio. When I got to his house he was on the porch, sitting comfortably in his dad's chair.

"Hey dude!" he hollered when he saw me, "are you ready for work?"

"*Dale gas!* Let 'er rip!" I responded, and he looked at me with a dumb look on his face. He didn't know what to say.

We went to the garage. We sanded and sanded. About that time, don Cristóbal came in.

"Okay, boys. Are you finished?"

"We're almost there, uncle," Patricio responded. "We're close."

After the primer dried we sanded all the dented areas again, but this time with smoother sandpaper. Then the final coat of paint was applied that matched the blue color of the car. Don Bernardo did the painting. Upon drying, it came out shiny—like new. Mike, Patricio's father, was happy.

"Good job, boys," he said. "Now comes the good part," he added, and he fetched his coin purse from his bib overalls. "Here you are . . . what did you say your name was?"

"Junie García."

"Open a hand," and I stuck out my right hand. "Here you are." He gave me six two-bit (twenty-five cents each) coins. "Whenever I have other cars to repair, come see me. Patricio will let you know."

"Thank you very much, Mr. Perea. I'll be seeing you."

"See you later, alligator," said Patricio, and I headed home, happy as a lark. I was anxious to show Mom the money before I chopped wood for her.

"Ah, hijito. Why so early?"

"We finished the work, Patricio and I. But look what I have, Mom," and I tossed the coins onto the kitchen table.

"Wow!" Mom exclaimed. "You're rich."

At that very moment Dad walked in, saw the money, and the first thing he said was, "What is this?"

"It's what Patricio's father paid me. What do you think, Dad?"

"Well, all that's good has a good beginning," Dad commented. "Now what are you going to do with your money?"

"Tomorrow's Sunday and I'm going to buy Nehi sodas for the entire family. I'm tired of Kool-Aid," I said. Mom smiled. "Whatever I have left I'll save in one of Mom's jars."

It wasn't long before the school year was over. Shortly thereafter, Mom and my little brothers and sisters and I left to spend the summer at the ranch. Dad had to work, and he visited us on weekends. The three months of vacation went by in a flash. Now it was time to return to Grandma's storage room to begin my second year of classes at Santa Barbara.

My teacher's name was Padilla, like my grandma's maiden name. Mrs. Padilla spoke Spanish as well as English. The first day of classes I ran into Patricio. We were going to be in the same class again.

"Hey, guy! How goes it, *ése*?" Typical Patricio jargon.

"Like all get out," I answered, and he burst out laughing. "And you, did you spend the summer sanding cars?"

"Off and on. There were few wrecks . . . little work."

That's the way the second and third school years turned out for me with the Pereas. I helped Patricio now and then on Friday afternoons or Saturdays. I earned my two bits, from time to time. As my second year at Santa Barbara School came to an end, Dad bought some property in Los Ranchos de Alburquerque to build the home he had promised Mom. On weekends I helped him load adobes onto his new truck. He purchased them from a man named Daniel Sedillo who had once lived in Martíneztown. From there we hauled them to Los Ranchos. Little by little Dad built the two-room house until he finished it (two more rooms came later).

Before my last year (the sixth grade) ended at Santa Barbara, Patricio came to see me one Friday evening. He was extremely happy.

"Hey Junie! There's lots of work. Can you come help me tomorrow, Saturday?"

"Come with me. Let me talk to my father." I went and asked him. He was drinking a cup of coffee.

"Okay, you may go tomorrow because next week school ends and we're moving to Los Ranchos. We will not be back." I looked at Patricio. He had a blank look on his face.

I went to help Patricio. Two cars were waiting for us, one a coup with two dented doors and another one with two really badly bent fenders. We worked without resting and finished everything a little before supper. Patricio's father paid me, and I thanked him.

"Look," said Patricio, "do you want to see where my uncle Bernardo applies the last coat of paint, after you and I finish? Come with me."

I had seen the large garage before; it was divided in two with a fine cloth curtain. We went into the first half. Don Bernardo was painting. He had on a mask that covered his nose and mouth. He was also wearing large plastic glasses to protect his eyes. We didn't put anything on. Don Bernardo didn't take long to finish a light blue car. Then he painted a strange-looking one, green and white. The third one was all red. By the time don Bernardo was almost done with this last car, I could barely breathe. The vapors from the paint were suffocating. I left the garage, covering my mouth and nose with both hands.

"Okay, Patricio. I'll be seeing you. As you know, next week we're moving to Los Ranchos. We won't be back." He didn't say anything. He had a sad look on his face.

I returned home and went inside coughing, with a hand over my mouth. Mom kept looking at me; she got scared.

"What's wrong, hijito? Why are you coughing? Did you swallow something or what?"

At that very moment a horrible cough overcame me, as though I were choking. All of a sudden I felt a slap on my back and I let loose gobs of spit in various colors.

"What's this, hijito? They look like rainbows!"

I didn't say anything. Some things are better left unsaid. At times that's much more mysterious.

Escupiendo arcoíris

PAT PEREA VIVÍA A unas cuantas casas de nosotros y cerca de doña Terencia. Él y yo nos hicimos buenos amigos después de un año en Santa Bárbara. A veces paraba por mí para ir andando juntos a clase. Estábamos en el mismo grado en la Escuela de Santa Bárbara.

Un día después de clase me acompañó Pat a casa. Yo traiba mis libros y lonchera, pero él no cargaba nada. Platicamos de muchas tonterías mientras que él le daba patadas a una que otra piedrita en el camino de tierra. Llegamos al frente de la yarda donde yo vivía.

—Ahi te wacho—dijo Pat—. Nos vemos mañana. Tengo que ir ayudarle a mi jefito en el garache—y se fue Pat. Luego se arrendó. —Oh, *by the güey*, ¿quieres venir alguna vez a camellar conmigo? Mi jefito y dos tíos míos componen carros que se han requeao.

Yo entendí algunas palabras, pero el resto de su palabreo me dejó rascándome la cabeza.

—¿Camellar? ¿Qué es eso?—le pregunté.

—Jale—contestó como si yo debiera entender lo que él decía.

—¿Y qué haces tú?

—¡De todo!—. Respondió de una manera vaga.

—¿Y trabajas por nada o te paga tu apá?

—Sirol, ése. Yo soy parte del negocio que él y mis tíos tienen. Con el jando que gano puedo ir al mono o lo que sea. ¿Qué dices? Si quieres le pregunto a mi jefito si puedes trabajar conmigo. Podemos hacer el jale juntos, tú y yo.

—Déjame hablar con mis padres. A ver qué me dicen ellos. Te digo mañana.

Esa tarde para la cena les conté a papá y a mamá tocante al trabajo con el papá de Pat y sus tíos. Lo primero que preguntó papá fue,

—¿Te van a pagar?

—Sí pero no sé cuánto.

—Pues bien, con tal que te paguen está bien conmigo. No lo vas hacer dioquis—dijo papá, y miró a mamá que estuvo de acuerdo.

Al día siguiente me topé con Pat camino a la escuela.

—¡Órale! ¿Qué me dices del jale?

—Me dieron permiso mis padres. ¿Cuándo puedo empezar?

—Este viernes después de la escuela si no estás ocupado. Ya hablé con mi jefito.

El viernes cuando menos pensé ya estaba por delante. Me acompañó Pat a casa al terminarse la clase.

—Ahi te miro al rato en mi chante pa que conozcas a mi jefito—y se marchó Pat.

Fui a casa y después de ver a mamá me cambié de ropa para partir leña o pompearle agua. No me tardé mucho.

—Ya estoy listo amá. Voy a ver al papá de Pat. A ver qué clase de trabajo quiere que haga yo.

—Ten cuidao hijito—me advirtió mamá—. Y está de vuelta pa la cena, antes que llegue tu papá.

Al llegar a casa de Pat, él me estaba esperando en el portal de su casa meciéndose en la silla de su padre.

—¡Órale! Qué pronto estás aquí.

—Sí, pero tengo que volver antes de la cena. Algo más. ¿Está bien si te llamo Patricio? Yo tengo un primo en Bernalillo con el mesmo nombre.

—Está bien conmigo. Es lo que me llaman en casa. Pat es el nombre que me pusieron las chavas en la escuela.

—Sí. Oyí a unas muchachas durante el recreo riéndose de tu nombre. Ellas decían PP (Pee Pee) en vez de Pat Perea, burlándose de ti. Yo sé lo que quiere decir eso. No es murre bonito.

—Ya sé quiénes son esas vatas. Se mudaron a Martíneztown de San Jo. Que me la pelen—vociferó Pat—. Vamos. Quiero que conozcas a mi jefito—y entramos en un cuarto mediano. Lo primero que vi fue un señal chico en la pared que decía Mike's Paint and Body Shop. En un rincón sentado detrás de una mesita estaba este hombre con cachucha y una mascada alrededor del pescuezo. Al vernos se puso de pie. Él era bajito y un poco gordo.

—Papá—dijo Patricio—, éste es Junie García. Él está en la escuela conmigo y vive cerca de aquí. Él me va ayudar a barrer y a limpiar los garaches.

—Muy bien, pero no quiero travesuras y que se vayan a lastimar—nos advirtió.

Él tenía un garaje bastante grande con dos puertas que se abrían y se cerraban como un acordeón, una para un lado y la otra para el otro lado. Entramos Patricio y yo. Él me enseñó el enorme garaje. Por dentro había una cortina negra de tela muy fina que dividía el garaje en dos partes.

—Éste es el primer garache. Aquí es donde mi tío Cristóbal, hermano de mi papá, compone los carros que le traen a papá que tuvieron un reque. Algunos vienen con puertas o *fenders* dañados. Mi tío Cristóbal sabe cómo enderezarlos. Después les pone primer y luego que se seca el primer me toca a mí. Yo raspo las puertas y los fenders con papel de arena antes de que mi tío Bernardo o mi papá los pinten del color del resto de carro. Ellos los pintan en el segundo garache. Los carros quedan como nuevos.

—¿Pero qué voy hacer yo, Patricio?

—Además de barrer los garaches, tú y yo vamos a raspar con papel arenoso las puertas de los carros o las partes que están atachadas. Ya verás. Yo te enseño cómo. Mañana sábado empezamos. Ven en la mañana.

Ese sábado como no había escuela pude dormir un poco tarde. Después de desayunarme dos rebanadas de pan tostado Rainbo y mi ollita de aveno con pasas, me puse mi ropa vieja que usaba para partir leña y otros trabajos en casa. Me despedí de papá y mamá y me fui andando a casa de los Perea. Llamé a la puerta del portal. Salió Patricio.

—Aquí estoy—y nos fuimos al primer garaje. Su tío Cristóbal ya estaba allí.

—Buenos días muchachos. ¿Listos pa trabajar?—fueron sus primeras palabras.

—¡Listos!—respondimos los dos a la vez en voz alta.

—Este carro nos vino ayer y como pueden ver estaba atachado todo este lado desde adelante hasta atrás. Yo ya le saqué las tachaduras y les puso el primer de pintura. Ora les toca a ustedes trabajar—dijo el tío de Patricio, y se sonrió—. Tienen que raspar las tachaduras con papel de arena hasta que queden lisas. Entonces se pintan las tachaduras del mismo color del resto de carro. Es lo que hace mi hermano Bernardo o el papá de Patricio. Bueno, Patricio, enséñale a tu amigo cómo se hace el trabajo—aconsejó don Cristóbal.

—Es fácil—dijo Patricio—. Yo empiezo con el fender y tú con la puerta. Mira cómo lo hago yo. Primero comienzas con el papel de arena más rofe y acabas con el fino. Aquí tienes los dos. Raspas de un lado al otro y luego de arriba para abajo. El fender—como dijo mi tío Cristóbal—, tiene que quedar bien liso.

—¿Tú has hecho esto antes?

—Desde el verano pasado. Ya soy un experto—acreditó Patricio con una risita.

Empezamos. Yo hice cómo me pidió Patricio. Me tardé buen rato. Raspé y raspé la puerta, primero con el papel arenoso, y acabé con el liso. Acaricié la puerta con la mano derecha; quedó bien lisita.

—Ahi tienes, Patricio. Ya acabé. ¿Qué te parece?—y vio mi trabajo como si él fuera mi patrón.

—¡Quedó a toda eme (ATM)!

—¿Y qué quiere decir eso?

—¡A toda madre!

—Me alegro—respondí aunque no entendí ni papa de lo que

dijo—. Bueno, Patricio. Tengo que irme. Mira el relo en la pader. Ya son las meras doce. Mi amá me dijo que volviera pal lonche.

—No se te olvide—me recordó Patricio—, todavía nos falta el fender de atrás. Te veo esta tarde.

—Bien. Vuelvo como a la una, una y media.

Me fui a casa corriendo para contarle a mamá del trabajo. Papá tuvo que trabajar ese sábado por la mañana; todavía no regresaba. Entré de prisa sin detener la puerta de alambre.

—Ah hijito. Qué gusto me da en verte. Pero mira cómo traes esas manos todas sucias. ¿Cómo te jue en tu trabajo?

—Me gustó. Raspé con papel de arena la puerta de un carro que tuvo un reque. Por eso tengo las manos tan puercas. Toavía nos faltó parte del carro. Esta tarde la acabamos yo y Patricio. Le dije que estaría de vuelta como a la una. ¿Está bien amá?

—Tendrás que ver qué dice tu papá. Él ya mero vuelve del trabajo. Anda. Lávate esas manos antes de comer.

Apenas acababa de sentarme cuando entró papá. Nos sentamos los tres a comer. Mamá tenía un caldito de papas y carne que había calentado. Mientras comíamos le pregunté a papá si podía ir a trabajar con Patricio esa tarde.

—Sí puedes pero no se te olvide que tienes que partir leña pa tu mamá cuando vuelvas. No dejes eso pal domingo.

—Güeno. Vuelvo pa las cinco—. Acabé de comer y me fui a ver a Patricio. Al llegar a su casa allí estaba en el portal sentadito en la silla de su papá.

—¡Órale!—me gritó al verme— ¿Estás listo pal jale?

—¡Dale gas!—le respondí, y se quedó mirándome con una cara de espantajo. No supo qué decir.

Llegamos al garache. Raspamos y raspamos. En ese momento entró don Cristóbal.

—Bueno muchachos. ¿Ya acabaron?

—Casi, casi tío—contestó Patricio—. Falta poco.

Después que se secó el primer volvimos a raspar todas las tachaduras pero esta vez con papel más liso. Luego vino la pintura final que hacía juego con el carro azul. Don Bernardo se encargó. Al secarse quedó relumbroso—como nuevo. Mike, el papá de Patricio, estaba contento.

—Buen trabajo, muchachos—dijo él—. Ahora viene lo bueno—y sacó él su portamonedas de la bolsa de sus pecheras—. Aquí tienes . . . ¿cómo dijites que te llamas?

—Junie García.

Abre una mano—y le puse la mano derecha—. Aquí tienes—y me dio seis monedas de dos reales cada una—. Cuando tenga otros carros que arreglar, vienes a verme. Patricio te avisará.

—Munchas gracias señor Perea. Ya nos estaremos viendo.

—Ay te guacho—dijo Patricio, y me fui contentísimo a casa. Me daban ansias de enseñarle el dinero a mamá antes de partirle leña.

—Ah, hijito. ¿Por qué tan tempranito?

—Acabamos el trabajo, Patricio y yo. Pero mira lo que tengo amá—y desparramé las monedas sobre la mesa.

—¡Híjole!—exclamó mamá—. Estás rico.

En eso entró papá, vio el dinero, y lo primero que dijo fue,

—¿Qué es esto?

—Es lo que me pagó el papá de Patricio. ¿Qué te parece apá?

—Pues todo lo bueno tiene su buen comienzo—comentó papá—. ¿Ahora qué vas hacer con tu dinero?

—Mañana es domingo y voy a comprar unas sodas Nehi para toda la familia. Ya estoy cansao de Kool-Aid—y se sonrió mamá—. Lo que me quede lo guardo en un frasco de mamá.

Faltaba poco para que terminara el año escolar. Poco después nos fuimos mamá, yo y mis hermanitos y hermanitas a pasar el verano en el rancho. Papá tenía que trabajar y nos visitaba los fines de semana. Los tres meses de vacaciones se pasaron en un decir amén. Ahora había que retornar a la dispensa de mi abuelita para empezar mi segundo año de clases en Santa Bárbara.

Mi maestra se llamaba Padilla como el apellido de mi abuela antes de casarse. La Sra. Padilla hablaba tanto español como inglés.

El primer día de clases me topé con Patricio. Íbamos a estar en la misma clase otra vez.

—¡Órale chavo! ¿Qué tal ése?—palabras típicas de Patricio.

—A toda eme—le respondí, y él soltó la risa—. Y tú, ¿te pasates el verano raspando carros?

—De vez en cuando. Hubo pocos reques . . . poco jale.

Así me fueron a mí el segundo y el tercer año escolar con los Perea. Le ayudaba de vez en cuando yo a Patricio los viernes por la tarde y uno que otro sábado. Ganaba mis pocos reales aquí y allá. Al acabarse mi segundo año en la Escuela de Santa Bárbara, papá compró un terreno en los Ranchos de Alburquerque para construir la casa que le había prometido a mamá. Los fines de semanas yo le ayudaba a él cargar los adobes en su troca nueva. Se los compraba a un señor Daniel Sedillo que más antes era de Martíneztown. De allí los llevábamos a Los Ranchos. Poco a poco fue construyendo papá la casa de dos cuartos hasta que la acabó (otros dos cuartos vinieron más tarde).

Antes de terminarse mi último año—el sexto grado—en Santa Bárbara vino a verme Patricio una tarde. Estaba rete contento.

—¡Órale Junie! Hay mucho jale. ¿Puedes venir a ayudarme mañana sábado?

—Vente conmigo. Vamos hablarle a papá—y fui a preguntarle. Él estaba bebiéndose una taza de café.

—Bueno, puedes ir mañana porque la semana próxima se termina la escuela y nos vamos a mudar a los Ranchos. Ya no volveremos—. Miré a Patricio. Tenía una cara de perplejo.

Fui a ayudarle a Patricio. Nos esperaban dos carros, uno de dos puertas tachadas y otro con dos *fenders* bien atachados. Trabajamos sin descanso y terminamos todo un poco antes de la cena. Me pagó el papá de Patricio y le di las gracias.

—Mira—dijo Patricio—. ¿Quieres ver dónde les pone la última capa de pintura a los carros mi tío Bernardo después que los acabamos tú y yo? Vente conmigo.

Yo había visto el garache grande antes; estaba dividido en dos con una cortina de tela fina. Entramos en el primero. Allí estaba don Bernardo pintando. Llevaba puesto una máscara que le tapaban bien la nariz y la boca. También tenía puestos unos anteojos grandes de plástico para protegerse los ojos. Nosotros no nos pusimos nada. No tardó mucho en acabar de pintar don Bernardo un carro azul claro. Luego pintó uno muy raro, de color blanco y verde. El tercero fue todo colorado. Ya para terminar don Bernardo este último carro, yo apenas podía respirar. El tufo de la tinta era sofocante. Salí del garache con las manos en la boca y la nariz.

—Bueno Patricio, ay te guacho. Como ya sabes, la semana que entra nos mudamos a Los Ranchos. Ya no volvemos—. Él no dijo nada. Se puso triste.

Volví a casa y entré tosiendo con una mano en la boca. Se quedó viéndome mamá; le dio miedo.

—¿Qué te pasa hijito? ¿Por qué toses? ¿Te tragates algo o qué?

En ese instante me pegó una tos feroz que no se me quitaba, como que me estaba ahogando. De buenas a primeras sentí un manotazo en la espalda, y solté dos o tres salivazos de varios colores.

—¿Qué es esto hijito? ¡Parecen unos arcoíris!

Yo no dije nada. Algunas cosas es mejor que se queden en el tintero. A veces eso es mucho más misterioso.

A Mysterious Woman

WORD HAD IT THAT doña Sabra was around fifty or sixty years of age. Nobody had seen her in years except for her son, Plácido, who cared for her. Mother and son lived in a two-story house next to the ditch that ran through the neighborhood. She had her bedroom on the second floor. From there she saw the water flow. That's how she spent much of her time since she didn't go out walking or anywhere else. Her husband and some of their friends had perished a long time ago due to a horrible illness that struck the community.

Doña Sabra's only visitor was her son. In the morning, he served her breakfast in her room before he went to work. In the afternoon, upon returning from his job, he went to see her. Later he cooked supper and both ate together in a small dining room on the first floor.

Plácido was about thirty years old or slightly more. He was a janitor at Saint Joseph's Hospital in Martíneztown. He worked five days a week—Monday to Friday—sweeping and mopping floors, and cleaning patients' rooms. He remained single to take care of his mother. I became acquainted with Plácido because I would see him from time to time at don Carlos Buenas's store, where he bought groceries.

Every Thursday Plácido, without fail, went to see don Carlos to purchase pork chops. Nothing pleased his mother more than diced crispy potatoes, fried zucchini, and oven-cooked pork chops. I found out about the pork chops by sheer coincidence.

On a very sultry summer day I went to don Carlos's small store to buy myself a cold soft drink to share with Mom. My favorite drink was Dr Pepper. I thought that, with a name like 'doctor,' it had to be healthy. I also liked Delaware Punch and Orange Crush. I learned to appreciate the three drinks after we moved to Santa Barbara.

"Good afternoon, Plácido. How are you?" Don Carlos asked.

"Everything's fine. From the house to work and back to the house . . . and taking care of Mom. That keeps me busy and out of trouble," and he smiled.

"Well, today is Thursday and I already know why you're here," remarked don Carlos. "I'm sorry, but the truck with the load of meats from downtown still hasn't arrived. Here I am waiting and waiting."

"Don't tell me. What am I going to do? You already know how much mother enjoys pork chops once a week. Without them she'll be very disappointed."

I listened to the exchange of words between Plácido and don Carlos while I drank my Dr Pepper.

"Let's see what I can do. Perhaps my friend Felipe García has pork chops at his store. If you want me to I can ask this young man to go see. This boy," pointing to me, "lives on this street not too far from don Felipe's store."

"As you wish, as long as Mom is happy."

"We'll see," said don Carlos. "By the way, this young man's name is Junie García. He can go in a hurry while you wait," he added, and don Carlos looked at me as I nodded my head yes. "Ask don Felipe if he has pork chops. If he does, have him send me four. I'll pay him later."

"Okay, I'll tell him," and I took off flying like at the ranch whenever my cousin Juan and I raced each other on foot.

It didn't take me long to get to don Felipe's store, which was close to the Santa Barbara Cemetery. He was the owner as well as the butcher. I went in. I found him behind the counter wearing a white apron.

"Good afternoon, don Felipe."

"What's up, Junie? How are you? And your grandma, is she all right? It's been a while since I saw her."

"She's fine, and so am I."

"Let's see. What can I get for you? Gum? Candy on a stick? Just say the word."

"No, nothing for me. Don Carlos sent me to see if you have pork chops. He ran out of them. He's got a neighbor who needs them for his mother."

"Ay Chihuahua!" he exclaimed, and he hit his forehead with the palm of his hand. "I'm sorry. The meat truck still hasn't come. I don't know why it's taken so long today."

"Thank you. I'll tell don Carlos," then I ran back to tell him. As I got there I saw a large truck with the name Swartzman, or something like that, in front of don Carlos's store. A tall, strong man was unloading sacks of meat.

"Don Felipe told me that he doesn't have pork chops," I informed don Carlos as I entered the store.

"Thank you, Junie. The meat truck has arrived," and don Carlos wrapped up some chops and gave them to Plácido. We both left the store together. He went to fix supper for his mom, and I returned to share my soft drink with Mom.

"Hijito, where have you been? I was worried about you."

"Mom, I went to don Carlos's store. Did you forget?" And I gave her what was left of the Dr Pepper. She took a swallow.

"Aaaah." She let out a long sigh. "This soda pop is really refreshing!" She took another sip. "I bet you don't know what we're going to have for supper? Something your dad likes a lot."

"Mom, I don't have the vaguest idea. Dad likes so many of your dishes."

"Pork chops!" she exclaimed.

"No, no. It can't be. That's why I took so long."

"Explain yourself, hijito."

"Well Mom, don Carlos sent me to don Felipe García's store to see if he had pork chops for doña Sabra, Plácido's mother, but he also didn't have any. Then the meat truck arrived at don Carlos. Now we, Plácido, and his mom are going to eat pork chops."

I could barely keep from laughing. But what was not a laughing matter, as I discovered little by little, was doña Sabra's isolated and mysterious existence. She spent her days in solitude, looking out of the window to watch the ditchwater flow—her favorite pastime. On cool days she liked to open the window to hear the water gurgling. Pigeons and other birds came, among them sparrows, to sip water.

At times she heard loud screaming. She'd approach the window and see boys who came to swim. Without suspecting that anyone was looking—or they didn't care—they undressed completely, yelled, and from the banks of the ditch jumped into the water. Doña Sabra thought it was funny to see them in the nude—and with so much energy and joy.

For days on end I didn't see Plácido. I worried that something had happened to him or to his mom. One evening after supper I took a short stroll. Their house was not far from where I lived. I knocked and knocked on the porch's door. Finally a disheveled Plácido showed up with his work clothes all wrinkled.

"Good afternoon. I haven't seen you in days. I came to see if you and your mom are okay."

"Gracias, Junie. We're more or less fine. With the fall season upon us and the cold nights it seems we have caught a cold. Last night this house was like an icebox because yesterday I wasn't able to chop wood for my potbelly stove or Mom's."

"If you wish, I can bring some wood from my house. I just chopped a pile."

"You're very kind. Pile it there on the porch. I don't want to wake up Mom."

I had been to Plácido's house several times but I had never seen doña Sabra's room—or her, for that matter. At times I would ask myself whether Plácido really had a mother or if they were just stories of his. All of that was a great mystery to me.

I went home and brought back wood in my dad's wheelbarrow. I did as Plácido asked me. I climbed three or four wooden steps and put the wood on the porch. I tried not to make a noise. I would come back next day to see how Plácido and his mom were doing.

I returned that Friday. I saw the pile of wood just as I had left it the day before. I knocked and knocked on the door, but there was no response.

I went in and saw Plácido sort of lying on a sofa. He heard me. His mother also heard me.

"Who is it?" she hollered from her room.

"Mom, it's the boy who brought us wood."

"Tell him to come here." Doña Sabra insisted on seeing me. Plácido did not object.

"Come in, come in, hijito," she said, and the first thing I saw was her face covered with a black mantilla like my grandma's. "What's your name?"

"Junie. Junie García. My grandparents have a house nearby. That's where my family and I live—in Grandma's storage shed."

"Plácido tells me that you're not from here in Santa Barbara."

"That's right. I come from Guadalupe in the Río Puerco Valley. It's close to where the Navajos live, but before long we're moving from here to Los Ranchos de Alburquerque. My dad is building a home there for Mom."

"Very well. I want to thank you for the wood you brought us. We almost froze to death the other night."

"Don't mention it. Okay, I have to go. I have to go chop wood for Mom before supper. That's something I do every evening."

"It was a pleasure meeting you. And come see me whenever you wish. I don't go anywhere. I'm shut in here day and night." I left while she sat in a chair with her faced covered.

That Friday evening as we ate supper Dad surprised all of us, particularly Mom, who was left speechless from sheer joy.

"Tomorrow we pack everything and leave for Los Ranchos. Our

adobe house is almost finished. It only needs plastering on the outside."

Dad looked at Mom and saw how happy she was. She was tired of living in that storage room cooped up like chickens.

On Saturday shortly after midday, we had everything practically packed and ready to go when I remembered doña Sabra.

"Mom, I have to go say good-bye to doña Sabra and Plácido."

"Come on, run!" and I took off flying like a jackrabbit. I got there and gave the porch door a few good wallops. Plácido came out.

"Today we move to Los Ranchos. I came to say good-bye to you and your mom." Doña Sabra heard my voice.

"Come on in, come on in, hijito. What a pleasure to see you. Don't tell me you're already moving."

"Yes. We're leaving today."

"Well, listen. If one of these days you come around here, stop by to see me."

"As you wish, but I have a favor to ask of you. No, no. It's not a favor. It's a question. How come you never uncover your face?"

"Look here. Or better said, pay close attention. On this earth evil tongues have wings. Do you understand me?"

"I think so."

"In other words, if I tell you why I have my face covered, sooner or later everybody's going to know. Do you understand me?" She repeated her question once again.

"But doña Sabra, how are people going to know if I don't say anything? My father has told us children that 'the gossiper pleases but he also angers people.'"

"Aha. With that bright response and precious face of yours I can tell that you're a very intelligent boy," and doña Sabra paused for a brief moment. "Many years ago there was what's called the influenza.[†] I was barely eighteen years old when I found out I was going to have a child. That's when Plácido, my only child, was born. A short

† The Influenza Epidemic of 1918 (a.k.a. the Spanish Flu).

while later that ugly illness struck me and left a lot of people dead, including my husband. Thank God I lived to be able to take care of Plácido. Now he's the one who takes care of me."

"But doña Sabra, why do you keep your face covered with that mantilla? Are you still in mourning or what?"

"Well, I'm going to show you a face that I guard like a secret. Only my son has seen it." She let out a long sigh and then slowly removed her mantilla.

Upon seeing her face, at first sight I was startled. She had what looked like pus-filled boils on her cheeks and forehead. Even a portion of her nose was missing. A chill ran through my entire body. The more I looked at doña Sabra, the more pity I felt. I started to sob in silence. Bit by bit tears came to my eyes.

"Don't cry, my child. What one sheds in tears you gain in sighing. And remember that on this earth, come what may, God gives and God takes away," and she crossed herself.

Una mujer misteriosa

SE DICE QUE DOÑA Sabra andaba por los cincuenta o sesenta años de edad. Nadie la había visto hace años menos su hijo Plácido que cuidaba de ella. Madre e hijo vivían en una casa de dos pisos al lado de la acequia que atravesaba por el barrio. Ella tenía su recámara en el segundo piso. Desde allí veía el agua correr. Así es como se pasaba las horas ya que no salía de paseo o a cualquier otro sitio. Su marido y algunas de sus amistades habían fallecido años atrás debido a una enfermedad muy fea que pegó por toda la vecindad.

La única visita de doña Sabra era la de su hijo. Por la mañana le llevaba él desayuno a su cuarto antes de que se fuera a trabajar. Por la tarde al regresar de su trabajo pasaba a verla. Luego hacía cena él y comían los dos en un pequeño comedor en el primer piso.

Plácido tenía sus treinta años o poco más. Él era conserje en el Hospital de San José en Martíneztown. Trabajaba cinco días por semana—de lunes a viernes—barriendo y lavando suelos y limpiando las habitaciones de los pacientes. Siguió siendo soltero para cuidar a su madre. Yo llegué a conocer a Plácido porque lo veía a menudo en la tienda de don Carlos Buenas donde él hacía algunas compras.

Todos los jueves sin falta iba Plácido a ver a don Carlos para comprar chuletas de marrano. Nada le gustaba mejor a su madre que papas picaditas bien tostadas, calabacitas fritas, y chuletas de puerco al horno. Yo supe de las chuletas por pura coincidencia.

Un día bien bochornoso de verano fui a comprarme una soda fría en la tiendita de don Carlos para compartir con mamá. Mi bebida favorita era *Dr Pepper*. Creía que con el nombre doctor tenía que ser saludable. También me gustaban *Delaware Punch* y *Orange Crush*. Llegué a apreciar las tres bebidas después que nos mudamos a Santa Bárbara.

—Buenas tardes, Plácido. ¿Cómo te va?—le preguntó don Carlos.

—Todo va bien. De casa al trabajo y del trabajo a casa . . . y cuidando a mamá. Es lo que me mantiene ocupado y fuera de problemas—y se sonrió.

—Pues hoy es jueves y ya sé por qué has venido—comentó don Carlos—. Lo siento pero la carga de carnes de la Plaza todavía no me ha llegado. Aquí estoy espera y espera.

—No me diga. ¿Qué voy hacer? Usté ya sabe lo mucho que le gustan las chuletas de marrano a mi madre una vez por semana. Sin ellas se va a desconsolar mucho.

Yo escuchaba el intercambio de palabras entres Plácido y don Carlos mientras me bebía mi Dr Pepper.

—Vamos a ver qué puedo hacer. Tal vez mi amigo Felipe García tenga chuletas en su tienda. Si quieres le pido a este joven que vaya a ver. Este muchacho—apuntando hacia a mí—, vive en esta calle no muy lejos de la tienda de don Felipe.

—Como usté guste, con tal que mamá esté contenta.

—Ya veremos—dijo don Carlos—. A propósito, este jovencito se llama Junie García. Él puede ir de prisa mientras tú esperas—comentó, y me vio a mí don Carlos mientras yo movía la cabeza que sí—. Pregúntale a don Felipe si tiene chuletas de marranos. Si tiene, que me mande cuatro. Yo le pago más tarde.

—Güeno, yo le digo—, y salí volando como allá en el rancho cuando echábamos carreras a pie yo y mi primo Juan.

No tardé en llegar a la tienda de don Felipe que quedaba cerca del cementerio Santa Bárbara. Él era el dueño como también el carnicero. Entré. Lo hallé detrás del mostrador con un delantal blanco.

—Buenas tardes, don Felipe.

—¿Qué hay, Junie? ¿Cómo estás? Y tu abuelita, ¿está bien? Hace tiempo que no la veo.

—Está bien, y yo tamién.

—Vamos a ver. ¿Qué se te ofrece? ¿Chíquete? ¿Dulce de palito? Tú dirás.

—No, nada pa mí. Me mandó don Carlos a ver si usté tiene chuletas de marrano. A él se le acabaron. Tiene un vecino que las necesita pa su mamá.

—¡Ay chihuahua!—exclamó él, y se dio una palmada en la frente—. Lo siento. Todavía no me llega la troca con la carne. No sé por qué se ha tardado hoy.

—Gracias. Yo le digo a don Carlos—y regresé corriendo pa decirle. Al llegar de vuelta vi una troca grande con el nombre *Swartzman* o no sé qué, delante de la tienda de don Carlos. Un hombre alto y fuerte estaba descargando costales de carne.

—Don Felipe me dijo que no tiene chuletas de marrano—le informé a don Carlos al entrar en la tienda.

—Gracias, Junie. Ya llegó la troca con la carne—y envolvió don Carlos unas chuletas y se las entregó a Plácido. Salimos juntos de la tienda, él y yo. Él se fue a hacerle de cenar a su mamá, y yo retorné pa compartir mi refresco con mamá.

—Hijito, ¿dónde has estao? Aquí me tenías con la pena.

—Amá, jui pa la tienda de don Carlos. ¿Qué se te olvidó?— y le entregué lo que me quedaba de la Dr Pepper. Ella tomó un trago.

—Aaaah—y dio un largo suspiro—. ¡Qué fresca está esta soda!—y tomó otro sorbo—. ¿A que no sabes qué vamos a cenar? Algo que le gusta muncho a tu papá.

—No tengo la menor idea, amá. Son tantas las comidas tuyas que le gustan a él.

—¡Chuletas de marrano!—exclamó ella.

—No, no. No puede ser. Por eso me tardé tanto.

—Explícate hijito.

—Pues amá, don Carlos me mandó a la tiende de don Felipe

García a ver si él tenía chuletas de marrano pa doña Sabra, la mamá de Plácido, pero él tampoco tenía. Luego le llegó la troca con carnes a don Carlos. Ahora nosotros, Plácido, y su mamá vamos a cenar chuletas de marrano.

Apenas aguantaba yo la risa. Pero lo que no tenía gracia, según supe poco a poco, era la vida aislada y misteriosa de doña Sabra. Ella se pasaba sus días solita, mirando la acequia correr por la ventana de su habitación, su pasatiempo favorito. En los días frescos le gustaba abrir la ventana para oír el gorgoteo del agua. Llegaban palomas y otros pájaros, entre ellos gorriones, a sorber agua.

A veces oía gritos fuertes. Se acercaba a la ventana y veía a muchachitos que venían a bañarse. Sin sospechar que alguien los miraba—o no les importaba— se quitaban ellos toda la ropa, daban sus chillidos, y de los barrancos de la acequia se tiraban en el agua. A doña Sabra le daba gracia verlos en pelotos—y con tanta energía y alegría.

Por días y días no vi a Plácido. Me dio pena que algo le había pasado a él o a su mamá. Una tarde después de la cena di un paseíto. Su casa quedaba no muy lejos de donde yo vivía. Toqué y toqué la puerta del portal. Por fin se presentó Plácido todo desgreñado y con la ropa de trabajo bien arrugada.

—Buenas tardes. Hace días que no lo he visto. Vine a ver si usté y su mamá están bien.

—Gracias, Junie. Estamos más o menos bien. Con el otoño por encima y las noches frías parece que nos hemos resfriado. Anoche esta casa estuvo como una hielera porque ayer no pude salir a partir leña para el fogón mío o el de mamá.

—Si quiere, yo puedo traer leña de mi casa. Acabo de partir una pila.

—Qué bueno eres. Apílala ahí en el portal. No quiero despertar a mamá.

Yo había estado en casa de Plácido varias veces pero jamás había visto el cuarto de doña Sabra o a ella misma. A veces me preguntaba yo si Plácido de veras tenía madre o eran nada más que cuentos de él. Todo aquello era un gran misterio para mí.

Fui a casa y traje leña en la carreta de papá. Hice como me pidió Plácido. Subí tres o cuatro escalones de madera y puse la leña en el portal. Traté de no hacer ruido. Ya volvería yo al día siguiente para ver cómo seguían Plácido y su mamá.

Regresé ese viernes. Vi la pila de leña en el portal tal y como la dejé el día anterior. Toqué y toqué la puerta, pero no hubo respuesta.

Entré y vi a Plácido medio acostado en un sofá. Me oyó. Su mamá también me oyó.

—¿Quién es?—gritó ella desde su cuarto.

—Mamá, es el muchacho que nos trajo leña.

—Dile que venga acá—. Doña Sabra insistió en verme. Plácido no se opuso.

—Entra, entra hijito—me dijo, y lo primero que vi fue que tenía la cara cubierta con una mantilla negra como la de mi abuelita—. ¿Cómo te llamas?

—Junie. Junie García. Mis agüelitos tienen una casa cerca de aquí. Es ahi donde yo y mi familia vivimos en la dispensa de mi agüelita.

—Me dice Plácido que no eres de aquí, de Santa Bárbara.

—Es verdá. Yo vengo de Guadalupe en el Valle del Río Puerco. Está cerca de donde viven los navajoses, pero dentro de poco nos vamos a mudar de aquí a los Ranchos de Alburquerque. Allí está construyendo una casa mi apá pa mamá.

—Muy bien. Quiero darte las gracias por la leña que nos trajiste. Por poco nos helamos de frío la otra noche.

—No hay de qué. Güeno, ya me voy. Tengo que ir a partir leña pa mi amá antes de la cena. Es algo que hago todas las tardes.

—Mucho gusto en conocerte. Y ven a verme cuando quiera. Yo no voy a ninguna parte. Aquí estoy encerrada día y noche—. Me despedí mientras ella seguía en una silla con la cara tapada.

Ese viernes por la tarde mientras cenábamos, nos sorprendió

papá a todos, en particular a mamá que se quedó sin saber qué decir del gusto.

—Mañana empacamos todo y nos vamos a Los Ranchos. Nuestra casa de adobe casi está acabada. Solamente falta enjarrarla por fuera.

Miró papá a mamá y lo contento que se veía. Ya ella estaba cansada de vivir en aquella dispensa como gallinas.

El sábado después del mediodía teníamos casi todo empacado y listo cuando me acordé de doña Sabra.

—Amá, tengo que ir a decirles adiós a doña Sabra y a Plácido.

—¡Anda, corre!—y salí volando como una liebre. Llegué y le di unos golpes fuertes a la puerta del portal. Salió Plácido.

—Hoy nos mudamos a Los Ranchos. Vine a decirles adiós a usté y a su mamá—. Doña Sabra oyó mi voz.

—Pasa, pasa hijito. Qué gusto me da en verte. No me digas que ya te vas a mudar.

—Sí. Nos vamos hoy mesmo.

—Pues mira. Si uno de estos días vuelves por acá, pasa a verme.

—Como usted diga, pero yo tengo un favor. No, no. No es un favor. Es una pregunta. ¿Por qué usté nunca se destapa la cara?

—Mira. O mejor dicho, pon buena atención. En este mundo las malas lenguas tienen alas. ¿Me entiendes?

—Creo que sí.

—En otras palabras, si yo te digo por qué tengo la cara tapada, tarde o temprano todo el mundo va a saber. ¿Me entiendes?—. Repitió de nuevo su pregunta.

—Pero doña Sabra, ¿cómo va a saber la gente si yo no digo nada? Mi apá nos ha dicho a nosotros los hijos que "el chismoso agrada pero tamién enfada."

—¡Ajá! Con esa respuesta inteligente y esa cara tuya tan preciosa yo sospechaba que tú eras un niño muy inteligente—y doña Sabra pausó por un breve momento—. Muchos años atrás hubo lo que se llama la influenza.[‡] Yo tenía apenas diez y ocho años cuando supe que iba a tener una criatura. Fue entonces cuando nació Plácido, mi único hijo. Poco después me pegó a mí esa fea enfermedad que dejó a mucha gente muerta, incluso a mi marido. Gracias a Dios que yo sobreviví para poder cuidar a Plácido. Ahora es él el que me cuida a mí.

—Pero doña Sabra, ¿por qué sigue con esa mantilla puesta sobre la cara? ¿Está usté todavía de luto o qué?

—Pues te voy a enseñar una cara que guardo como un secreto. Solamente mi hijo la ha visto—. Echó un largo suspiro y luego se quitó despacito la mantilla.

Al ver su cara a primera vista me espanté. Tenía como llena de granos enterrados los cachetes y la frente. Hasta le faltaba parte de la nariz. Me entró un escalofrío por todo el cuerpo. Cuanto más miraba a doña Sabra, más lástima me daba. Me puse a sollozar en silencio. Poco a poco se me vinieron las lágrimas.

—No llores hijito. Lo que uno derrama en lágrimas se gana en suspiros. Y acuérdate que en este mundo sea lo que sea Dios da y Dios quita—y se persignó.

‡ La Influenza Española de 1918.

SPANISH/ENGLISH GLOSSARY

The following words appear in the Spanish version of the stories and are listed here in case their meaning, subtleties, or pronunciation as we know them in New Mexico are unfamiliar either to the English-speaker who knows Spanish or to some Spanish-speakers themselves.

REGIONAL TERMS	STANDARD WORDS	TRANSLATION
acabates	acabaste	you finished
acafetado/a	café	brown
agüelita/o	abuelita/o	Grandma; Granny; Grandpa
ahi	ahí	there
ai	ahí	there
amá	mamá	Mom
amanecites	amaneciste	you woke up
ámonos	vámonos	let's go
anducio/a	vagamundo/a	rover, wanderer
apá	papá	Dad
asina	así	thus, thereby
atachao/a	abollado/a	dented
atascao/a	atascado/a	stupid; dense
atinates	atinaste	you hit the target
bos	autobús	bus
brel	pan (al horno)	homemade coarse bread

REGIONAL TERMS	STANDARD WORDS	TRANSLATION
calientito	calentito	nice and warm
cansao/a	cansado/a	tired
carrito (dim.)	carro	old clunker
ciudá	ciudad	city
comprates	compraste	you bought
creigas	creas	you believe
criatura	nene, nena	child
cuadril	cadera	hip; hip bone
cuasi	casi	almost
cuates	amigos	buddies/friends
cuidao	cuidado	careful
culeco/a	clueco/a	horny; brooding
culo	coño	pussy; cunt
chinelas	chinelas	slippers
chíquete	goma	chewing gum
chorizo	bolonia	baloney
chupar	fumar	to smoke
dejates	dejaste	you left (behind)
d'eso	de eso	from that
desgraciao/a	desgraciado/a	son of a bitch
dijites	dijiste	you said
dioquis	de oque; gratis	free
diputao	diputado	deputy
dispensa	despensa	shed (storage)
diun	de un	of a
dompe	basurero	dump
dormites	dormiste	you slept
elolote	elote	ear of corn
encadenao/a	encadenado/a	lined up
enfermedá	enfermedad	illness
en papá	papá	Dad; father
enterrao/a	enterrado/a	buried

REGIONAL TERMS	STANDARD WORDS	TRANSLATION
entrates	entraste	you entered
escusao	excusado	outhouse
espauda	levadura en polvo	baking powder
esqueroso/a	asqueroso/a	nasty, disgusting
estao	estado	(have/had) been
finación	fin	end; termination
garache	garaje	garage
güeja	cabeza	head
güeno/a	bueno/a	good
güevo	huevo	egg
hielera	nevera	icebox
íbanos	íbamos	we went, used to go
jalar	halar	to pull
jui	fui	I went
juites	juiste	you went
l'agua	el agua	the water
l'aroma	el aroma	the aroma
la cequia	la acequia	the ditch
lagañas	legañas	eye matter; bleariness
l'hacha	el hacha	the axe
l'ojete	fundillo	ass
lonchar	almorzar	to eat lunch
lonche	almuerzo	lunch
mala cacha	malo	cantankerous
mascada	bufanda	scarf
mesmo	mismo	same
mestro/a	maestro/a	teacher
mijo	mi hijo	my son

REGIONAL TERMS	STANDARD WORDS	TRANSLATION
mocho	medio alfabetizado	half-literate
muino/a	mohíno/a	grouchy
murre	muy	very
naa	nada	nothing
naide	nadie	nobody
naiden	nadie	nobody
nuevas	noticias	news
ojete	fundillo	ass; butt
ora	ahora	now
oyí	oí	I heard
pa	para	for
pacá	para acá	this way
pabajo	para abajo	downward
pader	pared	wall
pal	para el	for the
parquetito (dim.)	paquetito	small, tiny sack
parriba	para arriba	upward
pasates	pasaste	you passed
pene	centavo	penny (coin)
pescuezo	cuello	neck
pirujo	joto	homosexual
prender	enganchar	to hitch up (horse wagon)
puerco/a	sucio/a	dirty
queque	pastel	cake
reales	reales (moneda)	bits (two bits, etc.)
reló	reloj	clock, watch
renegar	decir palabrotas	to swear
repunoso/a	repugnante	hateful
reque	choque	wreck (car)

REGIONAL TERMS	STANDARD WORDS	TRANSLATION
requeao/a	chocado/a	wrecked
rofe	bruto	rough
sacates	sacaste	you took out
serruche	serrucho	hand saw
sobrenombre	apodo	nickname
tamién	también	also
tardates	tardaste	you took a long time
toa	toda	all
toavía	todavía	still, yet
tragates	tragaste	you drank
traiba	traía	s/he had (in his/her possession)
trastes	platos	dishes
troca	camioneta; camión	truck
trujo	trajo	s/he brought
túnico	vestido	lady's dress
usté	usted	you
vecindá	vecindad	vicinity
verdá	verdad	truth
viejo	querido	dear (noun)
volvites	volviste	you returned
yarda	patio	yard
zafao/a	zafado/a; loco/a	crazy

COMMON SPANISH EXCLAMATIONS AND EXPRESSIONS

¡A poco!	You don't say!
¡Cómo que no!	What do you mean "no"!
¡No me diga(s)!	Don't tell me!
¿Qué tal?	What's up?
andar a pie	to go on foot
cobrar un ojo de la cara	to charge an arm and a leg
comer como un barril sin fondo	to eat like a glutton
costar una pata y la mitá de la otra	to cost a pretty penny
dejar la botella	to give up drinking
dicho y hecho	better said than done
echar de contao	to swear (at someone)
en peloto/a	in the nude
en un decir amén	in the twinkling of an eye
estar hechos bolas	to be huddled together
hacer chile con la rosca	to get madder than hell
hacerlo dioquis	to do something for nothing

las malas lenguas tienen alas	evil tongues are poison
le falta una tuerca	s/he is crazy
meter chancla	to dance up a storm
no caberle un güevo en la rosca	unable to sit still
plantar un beso	to land a kiss
quedarse en el tintero	better left unsaid
se le fueron las cabras	s/he's gone bananas, nuts
sin pelos en la lengua	without mincing words
tener sus malas greñas	to have his/her bad side
trabarle los dedos a alguien	to give someone the finger; to tell someone to go fuck themselves
volteársele las muelas al revés	to get raging mad
y con buena razón	and little wonder

PACHUQUISMOS / ZOOT-SUITERS' VOCABULARY

agüitarse	to be a drag, a bore; to get mad or upset
camarada	pal, buddy
camellar	to work; to slave
cantón	home, house
carnal	bro, friend
compa	buddy
chante	home, house
chava	broad, chick
chavala	young girl
chucos	zoot-suiters
entabicar	to lock up in jail
fila	pocketknife
filero	switchblade
frajos	cigarettes
güisa	novia, sweetheart
jale	work
jando	bread; money
jefe	old man; father

jefito/a	old man; father; old lady; mother
jura	police
mono	movies
monquiar	to mess around
ruca	girlfriend
ruco/a	old man, lady; father/ mother
rucos	old folks; old farts
sirol	yes
tacuche	boy's suit (clothing); rags
trolas	matches (for lighting a fire)
vato/a	dude (male/female)

PACHUQUISMOS / ZOOT-SUITERS' EXCLAMATIONS AND EXPRESSIONS

¡A la chingada!	Holy shit!
¡A la vechia! (vequia)	Holy shit!
¡ATM! (a toda eme/a toda madre)	Out of sight! Like a bat out of hell!
¡Dale gas!	Let 'er rip!
¡Nel ése!	No way, man! Nothing doing!
¡Ni a tu madre!	Fuck off!
¡Órale!	Hey dude!
¡Órale chavo!	Hey kid!
¿Qué tal ése?	What's up, dude?
¡Sirol ése!	You got it! Of course, dude!
ahi te guacho	see you later
armarse la gorda	for all hell to break loose
dar la vuelta	to make the rounds
darle cuerda al reló	to get the lead out; to get going
dar un vuelazo	to hobnob
echar un palo	to screw; to have sex

ponerse de aquellas ponerse truchas	to get hip; to be cool to be on your toes
que me la pelen	they can fuck themselves
sonarse un leño	to smoke a joint
va haber pedo va haber retumbos	there's going to be trouble there's going to be a rumble